NINJA Foodi SMARTLID

Recipe Book

Simple and Tasty Classic British Recipes with Pictures. UK Ingredients, Metric Measurement and Coloured Pictures

INTRODUCTION

After a long day, nothing is more frustrating than realizing you *still* have to make dinner. Preparation, actual cooking, and the inevitable mess add up to a serious chore.

The Ninja Foodi can do most of the work for you. The Ninja Foodi has three cooking modes, 14-15 functions, and all of the accessories needed to prepare almost any meal. It's an air fryer, an oven, a hop, and more all combined into one handy pot. Furthermore, its pressure cooking mode reduces cooking time by 70%. (anything to spend less time in the kitchen).

This comprehensive recipe book goes far beyond what is covered in the Foodi SmartLid manual, providing delicious traditional British recipes with detailed step by step and clear instructions to help you master the Ninja Foodi SmartLid and cooking with confidence in no time.

WHAT IS THE NINJA FOODI SMARTLID, ANYWAY?

The Ninja Foodi is a "pressure cooker that steams and crisps." It's essentially an all-in-one pot.

According to its description, the Ninja Foodi is a "pressure cooker that steams and crisps." It's essentially an all-in-one pot. The Foodi features three cooking modes: PRESSURE, STEAM CRISP, and AIR FRY/HOP. It also has 14/15 functions that can make everything from fresh yogurt to loaves of bread. Here is the complete list:

- *Pressure*
- *Steam and crisp* (for making entire meals at once)
- *Steam and bake* (for baking cakes and quick breads)
- *Air fry*
- *Grill*
- *Bake*
- *Dehydrate*
- *Proof* (for helping dough rise)
- *Sear/sauté* (for using the pot like a hop)
- *Steam*
- *Sous vide* (for cooking food sealed in a plastic bag in a regulated water bath)
- *Slow cook*
- *Yogurt* (for pasteurizing and fermenting milk to make homemade yogurt)
- *Keep warm*

SO HOW DO YOU USE THE NINJA FOODI?

The nice thing about the Foodi's is that it cuts out some guesswork.

Using The PRESSURE Mode:

1. Open the lid, Insert the cooking pot.
2. Seal the release valve.
3. Move the SmartSlider to *PRESSURE* (The Foodi defaults to high pressure)
4. You will need to adjust the time before pressing the START/STOP button. Using arrow buttons, *set time for the recipe*.
5. Choose the desired pressure release: The unit will default to NATURAL RELEASE. use the dial to select between NATURAL, QUICK or DELAYED release (the recipe will state the required release method)
6. Press *START/STOP* to begin cooking.

Air Fry/ Hob Mode:

1. Open the lid,
2. Add Ingredients on the Deluxe Reversible Rack or Cook & Crisp Basket (as it will specified by the recipe).
3. Close the SmartLid.
4. Move the SmartSlider to Air Fry/ Hob. Once you've chosen a mode, use the dial to choose your desired function.
5. You can choose between : AIR FRY, GRILL, BAKE, DEHYDRATE, PROVE, SEAR/SAUTÉ, STEAM, SLOW COOK, YOGURT, KEEP WARM.
6. Using arrow buttons, set time and temperature for the recipe.

NOW IT'S TIME TO GET COOKING! TO GET YOU STARTED, HERE ARE SOME DELICIOUS NINJA FOODI SMARTLID RECIPES.

INDEX

Desserts

Egg Custard Tarts 8
Lemon Drizzle Cake 9
Burnt Cream 10
Madeira Loaf Cake 10
Treacle Sponge Pudding 11
Shortbread Cookies 11
Yorkshire Parkin 12
Strawberry Rhubarb Crumble 12
Golden Syrup Flapjacks 13
Lemon Curd 13
Lemonade Scones 14
Blueberry Scones 14
Rock Cake 15
Butterscotch Pudding 15
Pineapple Upside Down Cake 16
Lemon Curd Pie 17
Chocolate Fudge 18
Bread & Butter Pudding 18
Bakewell Tart 19
Spotted Dick 19

Breakfast & Sides

Kedgeree 20
Eggs In A Hole 20
English Muffins 21
Yorkshire Pudding 21
Courgette Cheese Egg Bites 22
Soda Bread 22
Haggis Croquettes 23
Onion Fried Rice 23
Haddock Fish Cakes 24
Poached Eggs 24
Jacket Potatoes 25
Egg & Asparagus Croquettes 25
Deviled Eggs 26
Frittata 26
Puffed Pancake 27
Leek Cheese Soufflé 27
Avocado Eggs 28
Cheesy Baked Eggs 28
Corned Beef Hash 29
Aubergine Dip 29
Bubble & Squeak 30
Broccoli and cheddar Omelet 30
Cheddar & Scallion Scones 31
Buttermilk Biscuits 31
Garlic Butter Knots 32
Cheesy Pull-Apart Bread 32
Goose Fat Roast Potatoes 33
Aubergine Parmesan 33
Hasselback Potatoes 34
Courgette Cakes 34

Beef

Lamb Stew 35
Irish Beef Stew 35
Beef Stew with Mushrooms 36
Oxtail Stew 36
Classic Roast Lamb 37
Roast Lamb with Mint Sauce 38
Shepherd's Pie 39
Scotch Egg 40

Standing Rib Roast 41
Birmingham Balti 41
Baby Back Ribs 42
Toad In The Hole 42
Beef Roast 43
Meatloaf 43
Rosemary Garlic Lamp Chops 44
Garlic Butter Steak 44
Stuffed Meat Loaf 45
Mongolian Beef 45
Sausage Rolls 46
Hash Browns Bake 46
Spaghetti Bolognese 47
Bangers and Mash 48

Poultry & Seafood

Chicken Pot Pie 49
Cornish Chicken Pasties 50
Chicken Parmo 51
Chicken Mushroom Pie 52
Chicken Tikka Masala 53
Chicken Rice Casserole 53
Chicken, Broccoli Rice 54
Honey Mustard Chicken Breasts 54
Hunters Chicken 55
Roasted Turkey Breast 55
Pizza Stuffed Chicken Thighs 56
Apricot Chicken 56
Grilled Chicken Skewers 57
Cornish Game Hens 57
Baked Chicken & Gravy 58
Chicken Stew 58
Creamy Chicken Soup 59
Chicken & Rice Soup 59
Butter Chicken 60
Tandoori Chicken 61
BBQ Chicken Legs 61
Stuffed Chicken Breast 62
Balsamic chicken 62
Fish and Chips 63
Creamy Fish Pie 64
Prawn & Tomato Stew 65
Cornish Crab Bisque 65
Prawn Fajitas 66
Cullen Skink 66
Prawn Tacos 67
Bermuda Fish Chowder 67
Creamy Cayenne Prawns 68
Honey Lemon Prawns 68
Maple-Dijon Glaze Salmon 69
Fish Chowder 69
Tuna Burgers 70
Lemon Pepper Baked Cod 70
Crispy Fish Fillets 71
Parmesan Crusted Salmon 71
Prawn & Vegetables 72
Coconut Prawns 72

Soups

Lentil Soup 73
Cauliflower Soup 73
Leek & Potato Soup 74
Squash Soup 74
Split Yellow Pea Soup 75
Tomato & Parmesan Soup 75

Egg Custard Tarts

Prep Time
30 Minutes

Cook Time
20 Minutes

Total Time
50 Minutes

Serving Size
12 servings

INGREDIENTS

Tart Crust:

- 180g plain flour
- 1/4 teaspoon salt
- 120g cold unsalted butter
- 2 tablespoons caster sugar
- 1 large egg yolk
- 2 tbsp water

Filling:

- 350ml milk
- 6 egg yolks
- 50g caster sugar
- 1 teaspoon ground nutmeg

Steps

1. In a large mixing bowl, add flour & salt. Mix until combined. Add the butter into the flour mixture, Mash with fork until resembles very coarse meal. Stir in sugar, egg yolk and water. Mix until dough just sticks together into ball. Wrap in clingfilm and refrigerator for 30 minutes.
2. In a saucepan over medium heat, add milk and heat until it starts to lightly simmer, Do Not boil. Remove from heat.
3. In a large bowl, add egg yolks and sugar and whisk until pale and bubbly. Drizzle hot milk into egg yolks while whisking.
4. Grease twelve (7cm) tart tins. Transfer the tart crust into floured surface and roll it. Use a 11cm fluted cutter cut circles. Place each circle in the tins and press to fit.
5. Fill each tart shell with custard and add a light sprinkling of grated nutmeg over each.
6. Add 240 ml water to the bottom of the Ninja. Place bottom layer of Deluxe Reversible Rack in the lower position. Place the tins on top of rack, then place rack in the pot.
7. Close the lid with valve is in the seal position. Select Steam Bake set temperature to 170°C, and time to 10 minutes. Select Start/Stop to begin cooking.
8. Then turn the temperature down to 165°C and Bake for another 10 minutes.

Lemon Drizzle Cake

Prep Time	Cook Time	Total Time	Serving Size
10 Minutes	*30 Minutes*	*40 Minutes*	*6 servings*

INGREDIENTS

- 70g softened unsalted butter
- 120g caster sugar
- 2 medium eggs
- 140g self-raising flour
- 1 tsp baking powder
- finely grated zest 1 lemon
- 1 tbsp lemon curd
- 2 tbsp full-fat milk

Icing:

- 250g icing sugar
- 3 tbsp water
- splash of yellow food colouring

Steps

1. Line a 20 x 20cm square baking tin with baking paper.
2. Using an electric whisk, beat butter and sugar together until pale and fluffy. Add eggs and whisk again. Add flour, baking powder, lemon zest, lemon curd and milk, and mix with a wooden spoon until all combined. Pour batter into the prepared tin.
3. Add 300ml water to bottom of Ninja Foodi. Place bottom layer of Deluxe Reversible Rack in the lower position. Place rack in the pot then place the tin on top of rack.
4. Close the lid with valve in seal position. Select Steam Bake set temperature to 170°C, and time to 25-30 mins or until a skewer comes out clean. Select Start/Stop to begin cooking.
5. Mix the icing sugar with just enough water to give a runny, icing. Put a small amount of icing in a separate bowl. Add a few drops of the food colouring to the icing until pale yellow. Spoon into a disposable icing bag.
6. Remove the cake from the tin. place cake on a wire rack. Spread white icing over top. Pipe thin lines of yellow icing across width of cake. Leave to set before cutting into slices.

Burnt Cream

Prep Time	Cook Time	Total Time	Serving Size
20 Minutes	*32 Minutes*	*1 hour 52 minutes*	*5 servings*

INGREDIENTS

- 6 egg yolks
- 6 tbsp sugar divided- 4 tbsp for custard, 2 tbsp for carmelizing
- 220g double cream
- 2 tsps vanilla essence
- 1 pinch salt

Steps

1. In a bowl, add egg yolks, 4 tbsp sugar, double cream, vanilla and salt.
2. Divide mixture evenly between 5-6 ramekins. Cover each tightly with tinfoil. (use tin foil wrapped all the way around the ramekin.)
3. Add 300ml water to bottom of Ninja Foodi. Place bottom layer of Deluxe Reversible Rack in the lower position. Place rack in pot then place ramekins on top of rack and Steam Bake at 150°C for 35-40 mins.
4. Remove hot ramekins and set on a rack to cool.
5. Once completely cooled, cover with plastic wrap and chill for 1 hour or up to 2 days.
6. When ready to serve, top each ramekin with 1 tsp sugar and then heat for 2-3 minutes in ninja to caramelize sugar. Let stand for a few mins before serving.

Madeira Loaf Cake

Prep Time	Cook Time	Total Time	Serving Size
15 Minutes	*35 Minutes*	*50 Minutes*	*6 servings*

INGREDIENTS

- 170g caster sugar
- 150g dried fruits
- 200g plain flour
- 125g softened butter
- 4 eggs
- 1 tsp baking powder
- Zest of one lemon

Steps

1. In a large bowl, add butter and sugar, lemon zest and beat with a hand mixer until light and fluffy.
2. Add eggs and beat for 4 minutes until combined. Add flour and baking powder and beat until creamy.
3. Add the dried fruits and mix.
4. Pour the dough into a greased 900g (1lb) loaf tin and cover with tin foil. Add 300ml water to bottom of Ninja Foodi. Place bottom layer of Deluxe Reversible Rack in the lower position. Place rack in the pot then place the tin on top of rack.
5. Close the lid with valve in seal position. Select Steam Bake set temperature to 160°C, and time to 15 minutes. Select Start/Stop to begin cooking.
6. Open lid, remove tin foil. Bake for more 15 minutes until toothpick inserted in center comes out clean.
7. Allow the cake to cool for 10 mins. Remove from tin, transfer to a cooling rack. Slice and serve with tea.

Treacle Sponge Pudding

Prep Time
10 Minutes

Cook Time
40 Minutes

Total Time
50 Minutes

Serving Size
4 servings

INGREDIENTS

- 100g butter, softened
- 100g caster sugar
- 2 medium eggs
- 100g self-raising flour
- 6 tbsp golden syrup

Steps

1. Grease a 1 litre pudding basin with butter. Put Golden Syrup in pudding basin base. Set aside.
2. In a large mixing bowl, Beat the butter and sugar until light and fluffy. Beat in the eggs one at a time. Fold in flour until it is mixed. do not over stir.
3. Scoop pudding batter into basin. cover the pudding with foil.
4. Add 300ml water to bottom of Ninja Foodi. Place bottom layer of Deluxe Reversible Rack in the lower position. Place rack in the pot then place the pudding basin on top of rack.
5. Close lid with valve is in seal position. move slider to COMBI-STEAM. Select Steam & Bake set temp to 160°C, time to 35 minutes until a skewer comes out clean. Select Start/Stop to begin cooking.
6. Open the lid, remove the basin, serve with custard.

Shortbread Cookies

Prep Time
10 Minutes

Cook Time
8 Minutes

Total Time
18 Minutes

Serving Size
8 servings

INGREDIENTS

- 6 tbsp Butter
- 50g icing sugar
- 100g plain flour

Steps

1. In a large bowl, add butter and sugar and beat with a hand mixer until light and fluffy. Add flour and mix to combine. The dough would be crumbly, do not over mix. Use your hands to bring the dough together to form a ball. Roll dough into a log. Wrap tightly in cling film and refrigerate for 30 mins.
2. Remove dough from the fridge, unwrap and slice into 1.5cm slices
3. Line Cook & Crisp basket with baking paper. Transfer cookies to basket. Place basket in ninja.
4. Select Air Fry, set temperature to 166°C for 10 mins. Let cookies cool for 5 mins in basket before transferring to a cooling rack with a cookie lifter to cool completely.

Yorkshire Parkin

Prep Time	Cook Time	Total Time	Serving Size
15 *Minutes*	1 hr 10 mins	*1 hr 30 mins*	16 *servings*

INGREDIENTS

- 120g medium oatmeal Stoneground
- 90g plain flour
- 1 1/2 tsp baking powder
- 2 tsp ground ginger
- 1 teaspoon allspice
- 1/4 teaspoon salt
- 180ml black treacle
- 60ml golden syrup
- 30g brown sugar
- 9 tablespoons butter
- 1 large egg , lightly beaten
- 2 tablespoons whole milk

Steps

1. Grease 20x20 cm baking pan and line the bottom with parchment paper.
2. In bowl, add flour,oatmeal, spices, salt and baking powder. Mix.
3. In a saucepan over medium heat, add sugar, treacle, golden syrup, butter. Heat until sugar is melted and remove from the heat. Let it cool for 5 minutes.
4. Pour treacle mixture into flour mixture and stir until combined. Add egg and milk and stir. The batter will be sticky. Pour the batter into prepared tin.
5. Add 350 ml water to the bottom of the Ninja. Place bottom layer of Deluxe Reversible Rack in the lower position. Place rack in pot then place the tin on top of rack. Close the lid with valve in seal position. Select Steam Bake set temperature to 140°C, time to 60-70 mins. Select Start/Stop to begin cooking.
6. Let the cake cool then invert onto a plate. Cut into squares and serve.

Strawberry Rhubarb Crumble

Prep Time	Cook Time	Total Time	Serving Size
7 Minutes	*18 Minutes*	*25 Minutes*	*5 servings*

INGREDIENTS

- 450g strawberries, (hulled & halved)
- 450g rhubarb, trimmed & cut into 1.5cm pieces
- 50g + 3 tbsp sugar, divided
- 6 tbsp unsalted butter, cut into small cubes
- 100g plain flour
- ¼ tsp salt
- 1 tbsp cornflour
- 30g almonds, chopped

Steps

1. In a bowl, add strawberries, rhubarb, 50g sugar and cornflour. Mix.
2. In another bowl, add butter and flour, rubbing together with hands until they resemble sand texture. Then, add 3 tbsp sugar, salt & almonds and mix.
3. Divide the fruit mixture among greased 5 small ramekins and top with the crumble mixture.
4. Place bottom layer of Deluxe Reversible Rack in the lower position. Place rack in the pot then place the ramekins on top of rack. Close lid and move the slider to AIR FRY/HOB. Select AIR FRY at 180°C for 18 minutes.

Golden Syrup Flapjacks

Prep Time	Cook Time	Total Time	Serving Size
10 Minutes	*12 Minutes*	*26 Minutes*	*8 servings*

INGREDIENTS

- 250g porridge oats
- 150 g unsalted butter
- 150g light brown sugar
- 2 tbsp golden syrup

Steps

1. Grease 20-cm cake tin.
2. In a saucepan over low heat, add butter, golden syrup and sugar . Stir until all milted and combined.
3. In a bowl add oats. Pour sugar mixture over oats, mix until all combined, then transfer mixture into the prepared tin. Press down until flat.
4. Place bottom layer of Deluxe Reversible Rack in the lower position. Place the cake tin on top of rack, then place rack in the ninja pot.
5. Close lid. Select Air Fry and set temperature to 185° C. Set time for 12 minutes.
6. Remove the lid and the cake tin. Place on a cooling rack. Let cool and then cut. Serve.

Lemon Curd

Prep Time	Cook Time	Total Time	Serving Size
7 Minutes	*13 Minutes*	*20 Minutes*	*12 servings*

INGREDIENTS

- 2 large eggs
- 2 large egg yolks
- 150g sweetener
- 125ml fresh lemon juice
- 2 tsp lemon zest
- 1/2 tsp salt
- 5 tbsp unsalted butter, (room temperature)

Steps

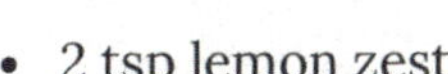

1. In a large mixing bowl, add sweetener, egg, egg yolks, lemon juice, lemon zest, salt and whisk well.
2. Transfer the mixture into a heatproof glass container. Cover with foil.
3. Add 240 ml water to the bottom of the Ninja. Place bottom layer of Deluxe Reversible Rack in the lower position. Place rack in the pot then place the glass container on top of rack
4. Secure lid with valve in seal position. Cook on high pressure for 3 minutes, Select DELAYED RELEASE and set time for 10 mins. Select Start/Stop to begin cooking.
5. Remove from Ninja, add butter to the lemon curd one tbsp at a time while whisking. Whisk until smooth and creamy.

Lemonade Scones

Prep Time	Cook Time	Total Time	Serving Size
15 Minutes	*15 Minutes*	*30 Minutes*	*10 servings*

INGREDIENTS

- 360g self-raising flour
- 240ml double cream
- 200ml lemonade
- 1 tsp vanilla essence
- Buttermilk, for brushing

Steps

1. In bowl, add flour, double cream, lemonade and vanilla. Gently mix until dough just comes together.
2. Transfer dough onto a floured surface. Knead until just smooth. Press the dough to a 2.5cm thick round. Cut out 10 scones.
3. Place scones on Cook & Crisp Basket. Brush top with milk. Place basket in Ninja Foodi.
4. Air Fry at 180°C for 15 minutes. Serve warm.

Blueberry Scones

Prep Time	Cook Time	Total Time	Serving Size
10 Minutes	*6 Minutes*	*16 Minutes*	*5 servings*

INGREDIENTS

- 180g butter slightly softened
- 250g plain flour
- 50g sugar
- 2 tsp baking powder
- 1 large egg
- 140g fresh or frozen blueberries
- 4 tbsp milk

Steps

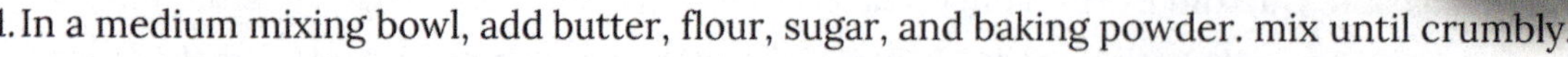

1. In a medium mixing bowl, add butter, flour, sugar, and baking powder. mix until crumbly.
2. Add in the egg, milk, one tbsp at a time, until the dough forms. Stir in the blueberries.
3. Roll the dough, until it is 1.5cm thick. Cut with 5-cm cutter into rounds.
4. Place scones on Cook & Crisp Basket. Brush top with milk. Place basket in Ninja Foodi.
5. Air Fry at 195°C for 5-6 minutes, until golden.

Rock Cake

Prep Time
20 Minutes

Cook Time
15 Minutes

Total Time
35 Minutes

Serving Size
4 servings

INGREDIENTS

- 240g self-rising flour
- 115g unsalted butter, room temperature, cut into pieces
- 1 tsp baking powder
- 1 tsp ground nutmeg
- ¼ tsp ground ginger
- ¼ tsp cinnamon
- ¼ tsp ground allspice
- 1 pinch ground cloves
- 4 tbsp brown sugar
- 5 tbsp raisins
- 4 tbsp dried currants
- 1 large egg
- 3 tbsp milk

Steps

1. In a bowl, add beat and 1 tbsp milk. Whisk.
2. In a large bowl, add flour and baking powder. Add the butter into the flour mixture, Mash with fork until resembles coarse meal. Add spices, sugar, dried fruits and mix until combined. Make a well in the center, pour egg & buttermilk and mix until just combined.
3. If the mixture remains dry, add milk, 1 tbsp at a time, until the dough holds together.
4. Divide dough into 12 rock-shaped balls.
5. Place cakes, well spaced out, into Ninja Cook & Crisp basket. Select Air Fry at 175°C for 15 minutes or until golden and well puffed.

Butterscotch Pudding

Prep Time
10 *Minutes*

Cook Time
20 *Minutes*

Total Time
30 Minutes

Serving Size
8 servings

INGREDIENTS

- 3 egg yolks, whisked
- 70g brown sugar
- 240ml double cream
- 2 tsp vanilla essence
- 60ml water
- pinch of salt

Steps

1. In saucepan over medium heat, add water and sugar and bring to a boil. Simmer for 3 minutes then remove from heat and add double cream. Stir then whisk in the egg a little at a time constantly whisking. Add vanilla and salt. Stir.
2. Divide mixture between 3 ramekins.
3. Add 350ml water to bottom of Ninja Foodi. Place bottom layer of Deluxe Reversible Rack in the lower position. Place the ramekins on top of rack, then place rack in the ninja pot.
4. Close lid with valve is in the seal position. Cook on high Pressure for 6 minutes. Let pressure release naturally.
5. Open lid, Transfer pudding to refrigerator until set. Serve.

Pineapple Upside Down Cake

Prep Time	Cook Time	Total Time	Serving Size
10 *Minutes*	10 *Minutes*	*1 Hour*	10 *servings*

INGREDIENTS

- 600g tinned pineapple slices in juice
- 12 candied cherries
- 4 tbsp melted butter
- 100g brown sugar

Cake:

- 180g plain flour
- 1 tsp baking powder
- 1/4 tsp Bicarbonate of soda
- 80ml milk
- 60ml pineapple juice , reserved from tinned pineapple slices
- 60g plain yogurt
- 1 tsp vanilla essence
- 115g butter, softened
- 150g caster sugar
- 2 large eggs, room temperature

Steps

1. In a 23cm cake tin, add melted butter, brush butter up to the sides of the tin. Sprinkle sugar over the top. Arrange pineapple slices and all the cherries on top of the brown sugar.
2. In a bowl, add flour, baking powder, Bicarbonate of soda and salt. Mix.
3. In another bowl, add milk, yogurt, pineapple juice and vanilla essence. Whisk.
4. In a third large bowl, beat the butter and sugar for 2 minutes with hand mixer until creamy and fluffy. Add eggs one at a time, while beating. Add 1/2 of flour mixture, mix using a spatula. Add 1/2 of milk mixture, mix. Add the remaining flour mixture, mix. Add remaining milk mixture, mix.
5. Spread batter over pineapple layer in the cake tin, smooth the surface.
6. Add 360ml water to bottom of Ninja Foodi.Place bottom layer of Deluxe Reversible Rack in the lower position. Place the tin on top of rack, then place rack in the pot.
7. Close the lid and move the slider to the COMBI-STEAM position. Select STEAM BAKE, set temperature to 160°C, and set time to 30 minutes. Press START/STOP to begin.
8. After 30 minutes, remove from Ninja, cover with tin foil, Bake for more 15 minutes until a toothpick inserted into the center comes out clean.
9. Remove cake from Ninja and leave inside tin to cool for 20 mins. Flip over the cake on a plate.

Lemon Curd Pie

Prep Time	Cook Time	Total Time	Serving Size
10 Minutes	*50 Minutes*	*1 Hour*	*6 servings*

INGREDIENTS

Pie Crust:

- 180g plain flour
- 1/2 tsp salt
- 115g butter or lard, cold & cubed
- 3 tbsp iced water

Filling:

- 300g caster sugar
- 4 small lemons , juiced and zested
- 4 large eggs
- 3 tbsp plain flour
- 1/4 tsp salt
- 4 tbsp unsalted butter ,melted
- 1 tsp vanilla essence

Steps

1. In a food processor, add flour, butter and salt. Pulse until mixture resembles large crumbs.
2. Remove food processor lid and gradually drizzle in water while pulsing, until mixture starts to form a ball and holds together. Don't over mix.
3. Transfer dough onto lightly floured surface. Knead until dough holds together without cracks. Don't over-knead. Then flatten into a 2.5-cm circle. Wrap in cling-film, refrigerate for 30 mins.
4. Remove dough from refrigerator and let it sit for 5 minutes. Sprinkle a large piece of baking paper with a little flour. Add dough on baking paper and sprinkle with flour. Roll out dough into a 30-cm circle, then transfer dough into a 22-cm quiche tin. Press down and trim the edges.
5. Top with baking paper, Fill with dried beans. Place quiche pan on the Ninja Foodi middle rack.
6. Close lid and move the slider to AIR FRY/HOB. Select AIR FRY and set temperature to 190°C. Set time for 15 minutes. Press START/STOP to begin cooking.
7. In a large bowl, add all filling ingredients and whisk until combined and smooth. Pour into pie crust. Place quiche pan back on the Ninja Foodi middle rack.
8. Close lid and move the slider to AIR FRY/HOB. Select AIR FRY and set temperature to 160°C. Set time for 40 minutes until top is set. Press START/STOP to begin cooking.
9. Remove from Ninja Foodi and let cool completely. Place in the refrigerator to fully set. Serve.

Note: You can use store-bought pie crust and start at step 5.

Chocolate Fudge

Prep Time	Cook Time	Total Time	Serving Size
5 Minutes	*7 Minutes*	*12 Minutes*	*6 servings*

INGREDIENTS

- 100g caster sugar
- 80ml water
- 110g butter, room temperature & cubed
- 350g chocolate chips
- 100g milk powder
- 1 tsp vanilla essence

Steps

1. In your Ninja Foodi, add sugar and water and stir.
2. Close the lid with valve is in the seal position and move the slider to pressure. Cook on high for 11 minutes. Use the arrows to select PRESSURE RELEASE and select QUICK RELEASE. Select Start/Stop to begin cooking.
3. Open lid, add butter, chocolate, milk powder, and vanilla to ninja, stir until melted and combined.
4. Pour/spoon the mixture into a lined 22×12 cm (2-lb) loaf tin and let it cool for 40 minutes, then transfer to fridge for 3 hours to set.
5. Lift from the tin, then cut into squares.

Bread & Butter Pudding

Prep Time	Cook Time	Total Time	Serving Size
20 Minutes	*6 Minutes*	*26 Minutes*	*12 servings*

INGREDIENTS

- 25g butter, plus extra for greasing
- 8 thick slices white bread
- 50g sultanas
- 2 tsp ground cinnamon
- 350ml milk, warm
- 50ml double cream
- 2 eggs
- 25g caster sugar
- nutmeg, grated, to taste

Steps

1. Grease an ovenproof dish. Spread each bread slice with on one side with butter, cut into triangles.
2. In the dish, arrange a layer of bread, then add a layer of sultanas. Sprinkle withcinnamon, then repeat the layers until all of the bread used .
3. In a bowl, crack the eggs, add sugar and whisk until pale. Add warm milk and double cream and stir. Pour mixture over the prepared bread layers, sprinkle with nutmeg and leave to stand for 30 minutes.
4. Add 360ml water to bottom of Ninja Foodi.Place bottom layer of Deluxe Reversible Rack in the lower position. Place the dish on top of rack, then place rack in the pot.
5. Close the lid and move the slider to the COMBI-STEAM position. Select STEAM BAKE, set temperature to 150°C, and set time to 30-35 minutes until set and golden brown. Press START/STOP to begin.

Bakewell Tart

Prep Time	Cook Time	Total Time	Serving Size
10 Minutes	*40 Minutes*	*1 Hour*	*12 servings*

INGREDIENTS

Pie Crust:

- 170g plain flour
- 2 tbsp icing sugar
- 115g cold butter, grated
- 1 egg yolk
- 2 tbsp water

Filling:

- 115g softened butter
- 100g caster sugar
- 2 eggs
- 150g ground almonds
- 1 tsp almond essence
- 100g raspberry conserve
- 25g flaked almonds

Steps

1. In a bowl, add flour, butter, egg yolk and sugar. Mix until mixture resembles large crumbs. Gradually drizzle in water, until mixture starts to form a ball and holds together. Don't over mix.
2. Transfer dough onto lightly floured surface.Flatten into a circle, transfer into a 23-cm pie tin. Press down, trim edges. Top with baking paper, Fill with dried beans. Place tin on Ninja Foodi middle rack.
3. Close lid and move slider to AIR FRY/HOB. Select AIR FRY and set temperature to 160° C. Set time for 15 minutes. Press START/STOP to begin cooking.
4. In bowl, add all filling ingredients (except conserve) and whisk until combined and smooth. Spread conserve over pastry base. Pour filling into crust, sprinkle with almonds. Place tin on Ninja middle rack.
5. Close lid and move the slider to AIR FRY/HOB. Select AIR FRY and set temperature to 155° C. Set time for 35-40 minutes until golden brown. Press START/STOP to begin cooking.
6. Remove from Ninja Foodi and let cool completely. Place in the refrigerator to fully set. Serve.

Spotted Dick

Prep Time	Cook Time	Total Time	Serving Size
10 Minutes	*30 Minutes*	*40 Minutes*	*8 servings*

INGREDIENTS

- 250g self raising flour
- Pinch of salt
- 125g shredded suet
- 80g caster sugar
- 1 lemon zest
- 1 small orange zest
- 150ml milk
- 180g mix fruit

Steps

1. In a large bowl, add all ingredients and whisk until combined. add more milk if needed. Transfer in a pudding dish, cover with foil.
2. Add 400ml water to bottom of Ninja. Place bottom layer of Deluxe Reversible Rack in the lower position. Place the pudding dis on top of rack, then place rack in the pot.
3. Close lid with valve is in seal position, move slider to pressure, select STEAM, set to 12 mins.
4. When cooking is complete. Move slider to Air Fry/HOB to unlock the lid, then carefully open it. Remove apples to serving plates. Serve warm.

Kedgeree

Prep Time *5 Minutes* | **Cook Time** *25 Minutes* | **Total Time** *30 Minutes* | **Serving Size** *3 servings*

INGREDIENTS

- 500g uncooked basmati rice
- 3 tbsp oil
- 1 large onion, chopped
- 2 tbsp curry powder
- 450g smoked haddock
- 600ml boiling water
- 6 eggs
- Salt & pepper to taste

Steps

1. Select SEAR/SAUTÉ and set the temperature to 4, add oil, onion and sauté until soft. Add curry powder, salt and pepper. Add rice and water. Stir, scrapping the pot bottom.
2. Place bottom layer of Deluxe Reversible Rack in the mid position. then place rack in the ninja. Place eggs on the rack.
3. Close the lid with valve is in the seal position and move the slider to Pressure. Cook on high pressure for 4 minutes. Select DELAYED RELEASE and set time for 4 minutes..
4. Remove eggs and place in a bowl of iced water for a minute, Peel the eggs and cut in quarters.
5. Add the fish to rice and stir until gently heated through. Serve with eggs.

Eggs In A Hole

Prep Time *2 Minutes* | **Cook Time** *8 Minutes* | **Total Time** *10 Minutes* | **Serving Size** *2 servings*

INGREDIENTS

- 2 slice bread
- 2 eggs
- Salt & pepper to taste

Steps

1. Brush both sides of bread with butter. Cut a hole in center of the bread.
2. Add 360ml water to bottom of Ninja Foodi. Place the bottom layer of the reversible rack in the lower position in the pot. Cover with foil, then add bread. Crack the egg into the middle of the bread.
3. Close the lid and move the slider to the COMBI-STEAM position. Select STEAM BAKE, set temperature to 160°C, and set time to 8 minutes. Press START/STOP to begin.
4. Season with salt and pepper and serve.

English Muffins

Prep Time	Cook Time	Total Time	Serving Size
35 Minutes	*15 Minutes*	*50 Minutes*	*7 servings*

INGREDIENTS

- 320ml lukewarm milk
- 1 sachet dried yeast
- 25g caster sugar
- 450g plain flour
- 1/4 tsp salt
- 2 tbsp butter

Steps

1. In a bowl add all ingredients and knead until a dough starts to form. Knead for 3 more mins until smooth. Cover with clingfilm and set aside in a warm place to rise until doubled in size. Roll out dough on a floured surface into rectangle 2-cm thick. Cut out circles of 8-cm. Cover with towel and leave for 30 mins to rise.
2. Add 360ml water to bottom of Ninja Foodi. Place the bottom layer of the reversible rack in the lower position in the pot. Cover with foil, then add muffins .
3. Close the lid and move the slider to the COMBI-STEAM position. Select STEAM BAKE, set temperature to 180°C, and set time to 11 minutes. Press START/STOP to begin.
4. When time is up, let cool then serve.

Yorkshire Pudding

Prep Time	Cook Time	Total Time	Serving Size
40 Minutes	*20 Minutes*	*1 Hour*	*7 servings*

INGREDIENTS

- 85g plain flour
- ¼ tsp salt
- 2 large eggs, room temperature
- 125ml warm milk
- 6 tsp oil or lard

Steps

1. In a mixing bowl, add flour and salt. Mix, then make a well in the center. Add eggs and milk. Mix until smooth. Allow to rest for 30 minutes.
2. Add a tsp oil in each hole of 6-hole tin. Place bottom layer of Deluxe Reversible Rack in the lower position. Place tin on top of rack, then place rack in the ninja.
3. Close the lid and move the slider to AIR FRY/HOB. Select AIR FRY, set the temperature to 190°C, and set the time to 8 minutes. Press START/STOP to begin cooking.
4. Crefully remove tin from Ninja Foodi and fill each hole with pudding batter ⅓ way full, then place rack in the ninja.
5. Close the lid and move the slider to AIR FRY/HOB. Select AIR FRY, set the temperature to 180°C, and set the time to 15-18 minutes. Press START/STOP to begin cooking. Serve immediately.

Courgette Cheese Egg Bites

Prep Time	Cook Time	Total Time	Serving Size
15 Minutes	*20 Minutes*	*35 Minutes*	*8 servings*

INGREDIENTS

- 4 button mushrooms, grated
- 1 courgette, grated
- 60g grated Cheddar
- 5 eggs
- 3 tbsp breadcrumbs
- Salt & pepper to taste

Steps

1. Squeeze grated courgette tightly to remove as much liquid as you can. Transfer all ingredients to a large bowl. Mix. Pour mixture into 8 silicon muffin cases.
2. Add 360ml water to bottom of Ninja Foodi. Place bottom layer of Deluxe Reversible Rack in lower position. Place muffin cases on top of rack, then place rack in the Ninja.
3. Close the lid with valve is in the seal position and move the slider to COMBI-STEAM. Select Steam & Bake set temp. to 180°C, and time to 20 mins. until the egg has puffed up and the cheese has turned golden on top. Press the START/STOP button to begin cooking.
4. Remove from Ninja and let slightly cool before serving.

Soda Bread

Prep Time	Cook Time	Total Time	Serving Size
10 Minutes	*25 Minutes*	*40 Minutes*	*8 servings*

INGREDIENTS

- 1 egg
- 1 tablespoon milk
- 500g plain flour
- 1 teaspoon bicarbonate of soda
- 75g raisins
- 300ml buttermilk

Steps

1. In a mixing bowl, add flour, bicarbonate of soda, salt, sugar and dried fruit. mix. Add buttermilk and stir. Bring together with hands then transfer dough to floured surface and form into a round loaf shape. Slash the top with a sharp knife.
2. Grease tin or pie dish that will fit in Ninja . Transfer dough to prepared tin. Brush top with beaten egg.
3. Add 360ml water to bottom of Ninja Foodi. Place bottom layer of Deluxe Reversible Rack in the lower position. Place the tin on top of rack, then place rack in the Ninja.
4. Close the lid with valve is in the seal position and move the slider to COMBI-STEAM. Select STEAM BREAD set temperature to 180°C, and time to 40-45 minutes. Select Start/Stop to begin cooking. (Loosely tent the bread with aluminum foil if you notice heavy browning on top.)
5. Remove the tin to a rack and let cool. Serve.

Haggis Croquettes

Prep Time	Cook Time	Total Time	Serving Size
5 Minutes	*20 Minutes*	*25 Minutes*	*4 servings*

INGREDIENTS

- 450g hot mashed potatoes
- 100g grated Cheddar cheese
- 4 tablespoons plain flour
- 1 large egg
- 100g cooked haggis

Coating:

- 1 egg
- 2 tbsp milk
- 60g plain flour
- 100g breadcrumbs

Steps

1. In a bowl, add all ingredients and mix until combined. Roll mixture into 20 finger-shaped croquettes.
2. Prepare three bowls: 1) flour 2) Beaten egg and milk 3) Bread crumbs and seasoning.
3. Dip each croquette into flour, then egg mixture, and then in breadcrumb.
4. Put croquettes in Ninja Cook & Crisp basket in a single layer. Air Fry at 180°C for 18 mins, flipping halfway through cooking time.
5. Remove from air fryer, serve.

Prep Time	Cook Time	Total Time	Serving Size
10 Minutes	*20 Minutes*	*30 Minutes*	*3 servings*

Onion Fried Rice

INGREDIENTS

- 2 tbsp oil
- 2 onions, chopped
- 375g uncooked basmati rice
- 700ml beef stock
- ¼ tsp garlic powder
- ¼ tsp garlic powder
- ½ tsp ground cumin
- ½ tsp soy sauce
- 2 eggs, beaten
- Salt & pepper to taste

Steps

1. Add rice and stock to your Ninja Foodi inner pot.
2. Close the lid with valve is in the seal position and move the slider to pressure. Cook on high for 4 minutes. Select DELAYED RELEASE and set time for 10 mins. Select Start/Stop to begin cooking.
3. Move slider to Air Fry/HOB to unlock the lid, then carefully open it.
4. Open the lid and fluff the rice with a fork. Transfer the rice to a bowl and set aside to cool off.
5. Move the slider to AIR FRY/HOB. Select SEAR/SAUTÉ and set temperature to 4. Select START/STOP, add oil, onion, once softened add garlic & saute for 1 min. Push ingredients to side of pot.
6. Add beaten egg and cook, stirring constantly, until the egg begins to set. Mix onion and egg until cooked through. Put the rice back into the Ninja Foodi and give all ingredients a good mix.
7. Turn off the Ninja Foodi. Add soy sauce and spices, mix and serve.

Haddock Fish Cakes

Prep Time	Cook Time	Total Time	Serving Size
30 Minutes	*10 Minutes*	*40 Minutes*	*4 servings*

INGREDIENTS

- 500g skinless cod/haddock fillets, chopped
- 250g peeled & grated potatoes
- 4 tbsp plain flour
- 2 tbsp dill & parsley, chopped
- Salt & pepper to taste

Steps

1. In a large bowl, add chopped fish, grated potatoes, dill and flour. Season with salt & pepper. Mix until combined. Shape into 8 patties, then let rest in the fridge for 30 minutes.
2. Spray Cook & Crisp Basket with cooking spray. Add patties on basket in a single layer coat with cooking spray. Place basket in pot
3. Close the lid. Select Air Fry, set the temperature to 190°C, and set the time to 5 minutes. Flip and Air Fry for more 4 minutes. When time is up, serve immediately.

Poached Eggs

Prep Time	Cook Time	Total Time	Serving Size
5 Minutes	*5 Minutes*	*10 Minutes*	*4 servings*

INGREDIENTS

- 4 eggs
- 8 tablespoons water
- Salt & pepper to taste

Steps

1. Grease 4 ramekins, crack one egg in each ramekin into it. Add 2 tablespoons water into each ramekin. Place ramekins in Ninja Drawers.
2. Add 360ml water to bottom of Ninja Foodi. Place bottom layer of Deluxe Reversible Rack in lower position. Place ramekins on top of rack, then place rack in the Ninja.
3. Close the lid with valve is in the seal position and move the slider to COMBI-STEAM. Select Steam & Bake set temp. to 182°C, and time to 4 mins.
4. Remove ramekins from Ninja, lift the egg from remaining water. Serve.

Jacket Potatoes

Prep Time	Cook Time	Total Time	Serving Size
15 Minutes	*30 Minutes*	*45 Minutes*	*4 servings*

INGREDIENTS

- 4 medium potatoes, washed and poked with a fork
- 1 tablespoon oil
- Salt to taste

Steps

1. Rub each potato with oil, then sprinkle with salt.
2. Add 360ml water to bottom of Ninja Foodi. Place bottom layer of Deluxe Reversible Rack in lower position. Place potatoes on top of rack, then place rack in the Ninja.
3. Close the lid with valve is in the seal position and move the slider to COMBI-STEAM. Select Steam & Bake set temp. to 190°C, and time to 35 mins.
4. Check potato doneness by poking potatoes with fork. If fork does not easily pierce potatoes, return to basket. Bake for another 5 minutes. Repeat until potatoes are ready.
5. Remove from Ninja and carefully transfer potatoes to chopping board. Slice potatoes down center.
6. Dress jacket potatoes with desired topping and serve.

Egg & Asparagus Croquettes

Prep Time	Cook Time	Total Time	Serving Size
30 Minutes	*15 Minutes*	*45 Minutes*	*6 servings*

INGREDIENTS

- 3 tbsp butter
- 3 tbsp plain flour
- 200ml milk
- 6 hard-boiled large eggs, chopped
- 65g chopped fresh asparagus
- 50g chopped scallions
- 50g grated cheddar
- 1 tbsp minced fresh tarragon
- salt & pepper to taste
- 80g breadcrumbs
- 3 large eggs, beaten

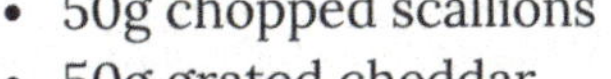
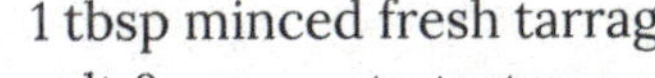
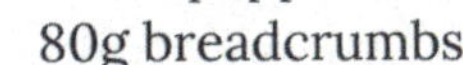

Steps

1. In a large saucepan over medium heat, melt butter. Stir in flour until smooth; cook and stir for 2 minutes until browned. Gradually whisk in milk; cook and stir until thickened. Stir in hard-boiled eggs, asparagus, scallions, cheese, tarragon, salt and pepper. Refrigerate at least 2 hours.
2. Shape egg mixture into twelve 7.5-cm long ovals. Place breadcrumbs and eggs in separate shallow bowls. Roll logs in crumbs to coat, then dip in egg and roll again in crumbs.
3. Place croquettes in a single layer on Ninja Cook & Crisp basket; spray with cooking spray. Air fry at 180°C for 10 minutes until golden brown . Flip; spray with cooking spray. Cook for 4 minutes.

Deviled Eggs

Prep Time 3 *Minutes* | Cook Time *15 Minutes* | Total Time *1 Hour 15 Minutes* | Serving Size *6 servings*

INGREDIENTS

- 6 eggs
- 3 tbsp mayonnaise
- ½ tsp chopped dill
- 2 tbsp pickled cucumber, finely chopped
- 1 tbsp smoked paprika

Steps

1. Place eggs in Ninja Foodi Cook & Crisp basket. Select AIR FRY, set temperature to 150°C and set time for 15 minutes. Then transfer boiled eggs into large bowl full with ice water. Peel eggs and cut in half.
2. In a small bowl, place the yolks. Add in mayonnaise, dill, and pickled cucumber. Mix and mash until combined.
3. Put it in the fridge for 1 hour to chill before filling egg whites. Spoon it into each egg white. Before serving sprinkle with paprika.

Frittata

Prep Time *5 Minutes* | Cook Time *20 Minutes* | Total Time *25 Minutes* | Serving Size *2 servings*

INGREDIENTS

- 4 large eggs
- 3 tbsp double cream
- handful chopped spinach leaves
- 75g feta cheese
- 80g cherry tomatoes, halved
- 60g diced red onion
- 1 tsp dried oregano
- salt & pepper to taste

Steps

1. Spray a 15-cm cake tin with cooking spray.
2. Whisk eggs and cream in a bowl. Add spinach, feta cheese, cherry tomatoes, onion, oregano, salt, and pepper. Mix until combined. Pour into prepared cake tin and cover with foil.
3. Add 360ml water to bottom of Ninja Foodi. Place bottom layer of Deluxe Reversible Rack in lower position. Place tin on top of rack, then place rack in the Ninja.
4. Close the lid with valve is in the seal position and move the slider to COMBI-STEAM. Select Steam & Bake set temp. to 180°C, and time to 12 mins. Serve hot.
5. Remove foil and Bake for more 6 minutes.

Puffed Pancake

Prep Time 5 Minutes | Cook Time 20 Minutes | Total Time 30 Minutes | Serving Size 3 servings

INGREDIENTS

- 3 large eggs
- 60g plain flour
- 120ml milk
- 1 teaspoons vanilla essence
- 2 tablespoons butter

Steps

1. Place bottom layer of Deluxe Reversible Rack in lower position. Place an empty 15-cm cake tin on top of rack, then place rack in the Ninja. Close the lid and move the slider to AIR FRY/HOB. Select AIR FRY, set the temperature to 200°C, and set the time to 5 minutes. Press START/STOP.
2. In a blender, add all ingredients (except butter) and blend until smooth.
3. Remove cake tin from Ninja, add butter to the hot cake tin and swirl it until melted and bubbly, pour pancake batter into the tin.
4. Add 360ml water to bottom of Ninja Foodi. Place bottom layer of Deluxe Reversible Rack in lower position. Place tin on top of rack, then place rack in the Ninja.
5. Close the lid with valve is in the seal position and move the slider to COMBI-STEAM. Select Steam & Bake set temp. to 180°C, and time to 15 mins. Serve hot.

Leek Cheese Soufflé

Prep Time 6 Minutes | Cook Time 8 Minutes | Total Time 14 Minutes | Serving Size 4 servings

INGREDIENTS

- 115g butter
- 1 leek, sliced
- 60g plain flour
- 2 tsp English mustard
- 300ml milk
- 100g Gouda cheese
- 4 eggs, separated
- Salt & pepper to taste

Steps

1. Select SEAR/SAUTÉ and set the temperature to 4, add butter, leek and sauté until soft. While continuously stirring, Add flour and mustard. Pour in milk and mix until thick. Season with salt & pepper.
2. Transfer mixture to a large bowl. Add egg yolks and mix until combined. Add cheese and stir.
3. In bowl, beat 4 egg whites until stiff and firm. Fold in egg whites in 2 parts into egg yolks/leek mixture.
4. Grease 6 240ml. ramekins and fill with soufflé mixture, leaving 1½-cm from top. Rinse the ninja inner pot.
5. Add 360ml water to bottom of Ninja Foodi. Place bottom layer of Deluxe Reversible Rack in lower position. Place ramekins on top of rack, then place rack in the Ninja.
6. Close the lid with valve is in the seal position and move the slider to COMBI-STEAM. Select Steam & Bake set temp. to 180°C, and time to 16 mins. Serve hot.

Avocado Eggs

Prep Time	Cook Time	Total Time	Serving Size
12 Minutes	*12 Minutes*	*24 Minutes*	*4 servings*

INGREDIENTS

- 2 avocados
- 4 eggs

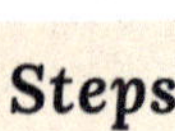

Steps

1. Cut the avocados in half lengthwise. Remove the pit. Carve out some of the avocado flesh.
2. Place the avocados on Cook & crisp basket. Crack 1 egg into the cavity of each avocado half. Season with salt and pepper. place basket in Ninja. you can add any additional toppings paprika or Parmesan cheese.
3. Close the lid and move the slider to AIR FRY/HOB. Select AIR FRY, set the temperature to 187°C, and set the time to 12 minutes. Press START/STOP to begin cooking.
4. Remove from Ninja and serve.

Cheesy Baked Eggs

Prep Time	Cook Time	Total Time	Serving Size
4 Minutes	*16 Minutes*	*20 Minutes*	*2 servings*

INGREDIENTS

- 4 large Eggs
- 60g Smoked gouda, chopped
- Salt & pepper to taste

Steps

1. Grease the inside of 2 ramekin . Add 2 eggs to each ramekin, then add 30g gouda to each. Salt and pepper to taste. Stir.
2. Add 360ml water to bottom of Ninja Foodi. Place bottom layer of Deluxe Reversible Rack in the lower position. Place ramekins on top of rack, then place rack in the ninja.
3. Close the lid with valve is in the seal position and move the slider to COMBI-STEAM. Select Steam & Bake set temp. to 180.°C, and time to 18 mins. Select Start/Stop to begin cooking. Serve hot.

Corned Beef Hash

Prep Time
5 Minutes

Cook Time
20 Minutes

Total Time
25 Minutes

Serving Size
2 servings

INGREDIENTS

- 450g red potatoes, peeled & cubed
- 1 onion, chopped
- 2 tsp oil
- ½ tsp smoked paprika
- 200g leftover corned beef, cubed
- 2 eggs
- Salt & pepper to taste

Steps

1. In a large mixing bowl, add potatoes and onion. Add oil, paprika, salt, and pepper. Stir. Transfer mixture to Ninja Cook & Crisp basket.
2. Close the lid and move the slider to AIR FRY/HOB. Select AIR FRY, set the temperature to 200°C, and set the time to 18 minutes. Press START/STOP to begin cooking. (flipping halfway through cooking time).
3. Open lid, add corned beef, mix. Air Fry for more 5 minutes.

Aubergine dip

Prep Time
5 Minutes

Cook Time
35 Minutes

Total Time
40 Minutes

Serving Size
4 servings

INGREDIENTS

- 1 aubergine
- 1 garlic clove, minced
- ½ green chilli, finely chopped
- ½ bunch fresh parsley, leaves only & finely chopped
- 1 tablespoon olive oil
- ½ lemon juice
- ½ teaspoon smoked paprika
- Salt & pepper to taste

Steps

1. Pierce aubergine a couple of times with a fork, then Place on Cook & Crisp Basket. Place basket in Ninja.
2. Close the lid and move the slider to AIR FRY/HOB. Select AIR FRY, set the temperature to 160°C, and set the time to 35 minutes. Press START/STOP to begin cooking.
3. Remove from Ninja and let cool.
4. Scoop the inside of aubergine, place into a bowl or food processor. Add all remaining ingredients and process/or blend with a hand blender until smooth.
5. Serve with bread.

Bubble and Squeak

Prep Time	Cook Time	Total Time	Serving Size
5 Minutes	*20 Minutes*	*25 Minutes*	*2 servings*

INGREDIENTS

- 1 kg maris piper potatoes, peeled & cut into 2.5cm pieces
- 500g mixed vegetables (carrots, cabbage, swede, turnips), peeled & cut into 2.5cm pieces. or you can use just cabbage
- 1 onion, finely chopped
- 400ml water
- Salt & pepper to taste.

Steps

1. Put the potatoes, vegetables, water and salt in Ninja Foodi.
2. Close the lid with valve is in the seal position and move the slider to pressure. Cook on high pressure for 10 minutes. Select Quick Release.
3. Open lid, Drain vegetables and transfer to a bowl, leave to dry for 6 minutes.
4. Season vegetable/potatoes with salt and pepper, then mash. Add onion and mix.
5. Roll mixture into balls, flatten slightly. Place on Cook & Crisp Basket. Brush with oil. Place basket in Ninja.
6. Close the lid. Select Air Fry, set the temperature to 190°C, and set the time to 20 minutes. Flip and Air Fry for 5 minutes. Serve.

Broccoli and cheddar Omelet

Prep Time	Cook Time	Total Time	Serving Size
5 Minutes	*35 Minutes*	*40 Minutes*	*4 servings*

INGREDIENTS

- 8 large eggs
- Salt & pepper to taste
- 300g broccoli florets
- 4 scallion, chopped
- 80g grated cheddar cheese

Steps

1. In a large bowl, add all ingredients and whisk until combined . Grease a 20-cm tin, then pour egg mixture into the tin.
2. Add 360ml water to bottom of Ninja Foodi. Place bottom layer of Deluxe Reversible Rack in the lower position. Place tin on top of rack, then place rack in the ninja.
3. Close the lid with valve is in the seal position and move the slider to COMBI-STEAM. Select Steam & Bake set temp. to 180°C, and time to 25 mins. Select Start/Stop to begin cooking. Serve hot.

Cheddar & Scallion Scones

Prep Time	Cook Time	Total Time	Serving Size
10 Minutes	*20 Minutes*	*30 Minutes*	*6 servings*

INGREDIENTS

- 1 egg
- 180ml buttermilk
- 240g plain flour
- 2 tbsp baking powder
- 4 tbsp caster sugar
- 100g frozen butter, grated
- 100g grated Cheddar Cheese
- 4 scallions, chopped

Steps

1. In a large bowl, add flour, baking powder, salt and sugar, mix until combined, add in butter, cheese and scallions and mix until mixture resembles small crumbs. Make a well in the center, pour egg & buttermilk and mix until just combined.
2. Transfer dough into a floured surface. Roll into rectangle. Cut into 12 round scones.
3. Add 360ml water to bottom of Ninja Foodi. Add scones in Cook & Crisp basket in a single layer. Brush with buttermilk. Place basket in ninja. Select Steam Bake, set the temperature to 190°C, and set the time to 15-20 minutes. When time is up, let cool then serve.

Buttermilk Biscuits

Prep Time	Cook Time	Total Time	Serving Size
10 Minutes	*20 Minutes*	*30 Minutes*	*6 servings*

INGREDIENTS

- 240g plain flour
- 1 tsp Bicarbonate of soda
- 2 tsp baking powder
- 1 tsp salt
- 100g frozen butter, grated
- A pinch of grated nutmeg
- 180ml buttermilk

Steps

1. In mixing bowl, add plain flour, Bicarbonate of soda, baking powder, and salt; add in butter and mix until mixture resembles small crumbs. Make a well in the center, pour buttermilk and mix until just combined. Transfer dough into a floured surface. Roll into rectangle. Cut into 12 round biscuits.
2. Add 360ml water to bottom of Ninja Foodi. Place biscuits in Cook & Crisp basket in a single layer. Brush with buttermilk. Place basket in ninja.
3. Select Steam Bake, set the temperature to 190°C, and set the time to 15-20 minutes. When time is up, let cool then serve.

Garlic Butter Knots

Prep Time
10 Minutes

Cook Time
15 Minutes

Total Time
25 Minutes

Serving Size
12 servings

INGREDIENTS

Dough

- 1 package active dry yeast
- 1 tsp sugar
- 240ml warm water
- 1/2 tsp salt
- 1 tbsp oil
- 300g plain flour

- 6 tbsp butter, melted
- 1/2 tsp dried oregano
- 1/2 tsp dried parsley
- 1/2 tsp garlic powder
- 1/4 tsp dried basil
- 3 tbsp grated Parmesan Cheese

Steps

1. In small bowl add yeast, sugar and water, mix. Let sit for 10 mins for the yeast to activate.
2. In large bowl add salt, yeast mixture and oil. Add flour gradually and knead until a dough starts to pull from sides of the bowl. Transfer into a floured surface and knead for 3 mins.
3. In a bowl, add melted butter, oregano, parsley, garlic powder, basil, and Parmesan. Mix.
4. Roll out dough into rectangle. Divide into 12 pieces using pizza cutter. Roll each piece into 13-cm rope, 2-cm thick. Tie each into a knot. Brush the knots with 1/2 of butter mixture.
5. Add 360ml water to bottom of Ninja Foodi. Transfer knots into Cook & Crisp basket in a single layer. Place basket in ninja. Select Steam Bread, set the temperature to 175°C, and set the time to 15 minutes until golden and cheese is melted. Press START/STOP to begin cooking.
6. Remove from air fryer, brush with remaining butter mixture and serve.

Cheesy Pull-Apart Bread

Prep Time
10 Minutes

Cook Time
4 Minutes

Total Time
15 Minutes

Serving Size
8 servings

INGREDIENTS

- 1 white bread loaf
- 8 tablespoons melted butter
- 3 garlic cloves, minced
- 100 grated Mozzarella cheese
- 50g Cheddar cheese
- 2 tbsp chopped fresh parsley
- 1 scallion, finely chopped
- Salt & pepper to taste

Steps

1. Cut loaf in a 2.5-cm grid pattern not slicing all way through.
2. In a bowl, add melted butter, garlic, parsley, salt & pepper, mix. Brush all bread loaf including the cracks with butter mixture. Fill the cracks with cheese. Sprinkle with chopped scallions.
3. Transfer bread into Cook & Crisp basket. Place basket in ninja.
4. Close the lid and move the slider to AIR FRY/HOB. Select AIR FRY, set the temperature to 175°C, and set the time to 4 minutes until golden and cheese is melted. Press START/STOP to begin cooking.

Goose Fat Roast Potatoes

Prep Time	Cook Time	Total Time	Serving Size
10 *Minutes*	35 *Minutes*	*45 Minutes*	*6 servings*

INGREDIENTS

- 12 small Maris Piper potatoes, peeled
- 1 tsp salt
- 4 tbsp melted Goose/Duck Fat
- 1 tbsp flour

Steps

1. In a bowl, add all ingredients and mix until all potatoes coated with fat and seasoning.
2. Place potatoes in Ninja Cook & Crisp basket. Place basket in Ninja. Close the lid and move the slider to AIR FRY/HOB. Select AIR FRY, set the temperature to 160°C, and set the time to 25 minutes until fork-tender. Flipping halfway through cooking time.

Aubergine Parmesan

Prep Time	Cook Time	Total Time	Serving Size
15 *Minutes*	15 *Minutes*	30 *Minutes*	4 *servings*

INGREDIENTS

- 2 medium Aubergine, sliced into 1 cm rounds
- 60g plain flour
- 2 eggs
- 150g breadcrumbs
- 1 tsp basil, chopped
- 500g grated parmesan

Topping:

- 400g tomato sauce
- 150g grated cheddar
- 50g grated parmesan
- Salt & pepper to taste

Steps

1. In a bowl, add flour, salt, and pepper. In another bowl, beat eggs. In a third bowl, mix together the breadcrumbs, basil, and Parmesan.
2. Coat aubergine in flour mixture, then in egg and finally cover in breadcrumbs until coated. Repeat for all aubergine.
3. Place aubergine in Ninja Cook & Crisp basket. Place basket in Ninja. Close the lid and move the slider to AIR FRY/HOB. Select AIR FRY, set the temperature to 185°C, and set the time to 10 minutes., flipping halfway through cooking time.
4. Open lid, top aubergine with tomato sauce then cheddar cheese. Close lid. Select Air Fry set temperature to 180°C, and time to 5 minutes.
5. Serve with pasta.

Hasselback Potatoes

Prep Time	Cook Time	Total Time	Serving Size
10 Minutes	*40 Minutes*	*50 Minutes*	*4 servings*

INGREDIENTS

- 1 kg small Maris Piper potatoes
- Melted butter
- Salt & pepper to taste
- 1 tsp rosemary or oregano (optional)

Steps

1. Place a potato on a chopping board between 2 wooden spoons handles. Cut slits 1/2-cm apart in potatoes, leaving the bottom intact. Drizzle with oil, season with salt & pepper.
2. Arrange the potatoes in Ninja Cook & Crisp basket. Place basket in Ninja.
3. Close the lid and move the slider to AIR FRY/HOB. Select AIR FRY, set the temperature to 180°C, and set the time to 30 minutes. (flipping halfway through cooking time)
4. Open lid and brush each potato with butter, then Air Fry for a further 5 minutes, or until golden, crisp and tender.

Courgette Cakes

Prep Time	Cook Time	Total Time	Serving Size
15 Minutes	*15 Minutes*	*30 Minutes*	*4 servings*

INGREDIENTS

- 2 medium courgettes, grated
- 1 lemon, juice and zest
- 2 egg, beaten
- 100 g plain flour
- 100g your favourite grated cheese
- 1 tsp dried oregano
- Salt & pepper to taste

Steps

1. Squeeze out as much water as you can from courgettes. Transfer to a large bowl. Add all remaining ingredients. Mix. Shape the mixture into 12 patties.
2. Transfer patties to Ninja Cook & Crisp basket and spray with cooking spray. Place basket in Ninja.
3. Close the lid and move the slider to AIR FRY/HOB. Select AIR FRY, set the temperature to 190°C, and set the time to 12 minutes. (flipping halfway through cooking time)

Lamb Stew

Prep Time *10 Minutes* | Cook Time *40 Minutes* | Total Time *50 Minutes* | Serving Size *6 servings*

INGREDIENTS

- 1 kg lamb shoulder, trimmed & cubed
- 1 tbsp oil
- 1 kg potatoes, peeled & chopped
- 2 onions, chopped
- 2 carrots, peeled & chopped
- 1 turnip, peeled & chopped
- 1 tsp dried thyme
- 1 1/2 litre lamb stock
- Salt & pepper to taste

Steps

1. Select SEAR/SAUTÉ and set the temperature to HI-5, add oil and cook meat until browned on all sides. Add the onion and sauté for 1 minute. Add all remaining ingredients and stir, scrapping the bottom of the pot.
2. Close the lid with valve is in the seal position. Cook on high pressure for 30 minutes. Select DELAYED RELEASE and set time for 10 mins. Select Start/Stop to begin cooking.
3. Serve.

Irish Beef Stew

Prep Time *5 Minutes* | Cook Time *35 Minutes* | Total Time *40 Minutes* | Serving Size *8 servings*

INGREDIENTS

- 1 kg stewing beef, cubed
- 1 tbsp oil
- 1 kg potatoes, peeled & chopped
- 2 onions, chopped
- 18 button mushrooms, left whole
- 2 carrots, peeled & chopped
- 1 turnip, peeled & chopped
- 1 tsp dried thyme
- 1 1/2 litre beef stock
- Salt & pepper to taste

Steps

1. Select SEAR/SAUTÉ and set the temperature to 5, add oil and cook meat until browned on all sides. Add all remaining ingredients (except mushrooms, carrots and potatoes).
2. Close the lid with valve is in the seal position. Cook on high pressure for 30 minutes. Select Quick Release.
3. Open lid, add mushrooms, potatoes and carrots. Close lid and cook on high pressure for 4 minutes. Select Quick Release.
4. Serve warm with bread.

Beef Stew with Mushrooms

Prep Time	**Cook Time**	**Total Time**	**Serving Size**
10 Minutes	***30 Mins***	***40 Mins***	***4 servings***

INGREDIENTS

- 700g boneless braising steak, cubed
- 2 cloves garlic, minced
- 2 stalks celery, sliced
- 250g mushrooms, cut into halves
- 600ml water
- 4 carrots, chopped
- 2 potatoes, cubed
- Salt & pepper to taste

Steps

1. Move the slider to AIR FRY/HOB. Select SEAR/SAUTÉ and set the temperature to 5. Select START/STOP, add oil Brown the cubed beef (working in patches) , adding more oil as needed. Using a slotted spoon, remove browned beef from the pot and transfer it into a plate.
2. Add garlic and celery, and stir, cook for 1-2 minutes. Return the meat to pot. Add in mushrooms and water. Season with salt and pepper.
3. Close lid. cook on high pressure for 17 mins. Select QUICK RELEASE. Select Start/Stop to begin cooking.
4. Move slider to Air Fry/HOB to unlock the lid,and add carrots, and potatoes to the pot. Secure lid with valve in seal position and cook on high pressure for 5 minutes. Select QUICK RELEASE.
5. Open the lid and adjust seasoning as needed. Serve.

Oxtail Stew

Prep Time	**Cook Time**	**Total Time**	**Serving Size**
20 Minutes	***40 Minutes***	***1 Hour***	***6 servings***

INGREDIENTS

- 1.3kg oxtail, cut into chunks
- 3 tbsp plain flour
- 3tbsp soil
- 2 onions, chopped
- 2 garlic cloves, minced
- 2 carrots, finely chopped
- 2 celery stalks, finely chopped
- ½ tsp dried thyme
- 2 bay leaves
- 400ml beef stock
- 3 tbsp tomato concentrate
- 1.5 tablespoon soy sauce
- Salt & pepper to taste

Steps

1. Move the slider to AIR FRY/HOB. Select SEAR/SAUTÉ and set the temperature to 5. Select START/STOP, add oil, brown oxtail in batches and transfer to bowl. Add more oil, Add in onions, then saute for 2 mins. Add in tomato concentrate, bay leaves, thyme. Saute for 3 mins. Add in garlic, then saute for minute. Add all ingredients to Ninja Foodi pot. Stir, scrapping the bottom of the pot.
2. Close lid and cook on high pressure for 40 mins. Select DELAYED RELEASE and set time for 20 mins. Select Start/Stop to begin cooking. Move slider to Air Fry/HOB to unlock the lid, then carefully open it. Adjust seasoning and serve with potato mash or rice.

Classic Roast Lamb

Prep Time
10 Minutes

Cook Time
45 Minutes

Total Time
55 Minutes

Serving Size
4 servings

INGREDIENTS

- 1 kg leg lamb, room temperature, fat trimmed
- 2 garlic cloves, crushed
- 1 tbsp chopped fresh rosemary leaves
- 1 kg potatoes, halved
- 60ml olive oil

Steps

1. In a bowl, add garlic, oil, oregano and rosemary. Mix. Rub half oil mixture over lamb and potatoes. Season with salt & pepper.
2. Add 350ml water to bottom of Ninja Foodi. Add Foodi Cook & Crisp basket in, add lamb leg and potatoes in the basket.
3. Close the lid with valve is in the seal position and move the slider to pressure. Cook on high for 30 minutes. Select Start/Stop to begin cooking. Select DELAYED RELEASE and set time for 3 mins. Select Start/Stop to begin cooking.
4. Open the lid, then Brush remaining half oil mixture over lamb and potatoes.
5. Close the lid with valve is in the seal position . Select Air Crisp/Air Fry set temperature to 200°C, and time to 8 minutes.
6. When cooking is complete, remove the basket from the pot and leave to rest on a plate, covering loosely with tin foil.
7. To serve, carve the lamb and serve with potatoes.

Roast Lamb with Mint Sauce

INGREDIENTS

Lamb

- 1.4 kg boneless lamb leg
- 3 garlic cloves, sliced
- 2 tbsp oil
- Salt & pepper to taste

Mint Sauce

- 30g mint leaves, finely chopped
- 2 tbsp brown sugar
- 2 ½ tbsp vinegar
- 2 tbsp boiling water
- 1 tsp salt

Prep Time	Cook Time	Total Time	Serving Size
4 Minutes	*60 Minutes*	*64 Minutes*	*4 servings*

Steps

1. With a sharp knife cut 2-cm long slits into the lamb skin. Insert one garlic piece into each slit. Coat the lamb with oil and season with salt & pepper.
2. Add 250ml water to bottom of Ninja Foodi. Place bottom layer of Deluxe Reversible Rack in the lower position. Place the lamb on top of rack, then place rack in the ninja pot.
3. Close the lid with valve is in the seal position and move the slider to COMBI-STEAM. Select Steam & Bake set temperature to 180°C, and time to 20 minutes. Select Start/Stop to begin cooking.
4. In small bowl, add water, mint leaves, vinegar, sugar and salt, stir set aside.
5. After 20 mins. remove lamb from Ninja Foodi, and rub the mint sauce over the entire lamb. Place lamb back on the rack in the ninja pot.
6. Close the lid with valve is in the seal position and move the slider to COMBI-STEAM. Select Steam & Bake set temperature to 180°C, and time to 20 minutes. Select Start/Stop to begin cooking. Repeat process 1 more time and cook for a last 20 mins.
7. Remove from Ninja, wrap lamb leg in tin foil and let rest for 10 mins. Slice and serve.

Shepherd's Pie

Total Time 1 1/2 Hours

Serving Size *6 servings*

INGREDIENTS

- 1 tsp oil
- 1 large onion, chopped
- 2 large carrots, chopped
- 2 large mushrooms, chopped
- 1 clove garlic, minced
- 450g lamb mince
- 1 (300g) tin chopped tomato
- 1 beef stock cube
- 100 g Frozen Peas
- 2 tbsp tomato puree
- 1 tbsp cornflour mixed with 1 tbsp water

For the mash:

- 800g small potatoes
- 200ml double cream
- 100g butter

Steps

1. Move the slider to AIR FRY/HOB. Select SEAR/SAUTÉ and set the temperature to HI-5. Select START/STOP, add oil, onion, once softened add garlic and mince. cook until browned. Add carrots, mushrooms, tomatoes & puree, beef stock, salt & pepper. Close lid and cook on high pressure for 3 mins. Use the arrows to select PRESSURE RELEASE and select QUICK RELEASE. elect Start/Stop to begin cooking.
2. Move the slider to AIR FRY/HOB. Select SEAR/SAUTÉ and set the temperature to 4. Add cornflour mixture, simmer until thickened.
3. Grease a 23-cm deep pie dish. Add mince mixture into the pie dish. Set aside.
4. Rinse the Ninja Foodi pot. Put the potatoes, water and salt in Ninja Foodi pot.
5. Close the lid with valve is in the seal position and move the slider to pressure. Cook on high for 10 minutes. Use the arrows to select PRESSURE RELEASE and select QUICK RELEASE. Select Start/Stop to begin cooking. Move slider to Air Fry/HOB to unlock the lid, then carefully open it.
6. Drain and add the double cream, butter, and pepper to the Ninja Foodi.
7. Use a potato masher to mash the potatoes, add more salt and double cream if necessary.
8. Spread mashed potatoes evenly over the mince mixture.
9. Add 240ml water to bottom of Ninja Foodi. Place bottom layer of Deluxe Reversible Rack in the lower position. Place the dish on top of rack, then place rack in the pot.
10. Close the lid with valve is in the seal position and move the slider to COMBI-STEAM. Select Steam & Crisp set temperature to 180°C, and time to 35 minutes. Select Start/Stop to begin cooking.
11. Serve hot.

Scotch Egg

Prep Time	Cook Time	Total Time	Serving Size
15 Minutes	*25 Minutes*	*40 Minutes*	*4 servings*

INGREDIENTS

- 450g minced beef, (90% lean)
- 5 eggs, divided
- 1 tsp. dried sage
- 1/2 tsp red chili flake
- 1/2 tsp garlic powder
- 1/2 tsp onion powder
- 60g plain flour
- 2 tbsp milk
- 60g breadcrumbs
- Salt & pepper to taste

Steps

1. In medium saucepan over high heat. bring 1 liter of water to a boil; add 4 eggs, boil 5 minutes. Then transfer boiled eggs into a large bowl full with ice water. Peel the eggs.
2. In a large mixing bowl, add minced beef, all the spices and season with salt & pepper. Mix until all combined. Divide the minced beef into 4 portions and form into ½cm thick disks. Place the egg in the middle of each disk. Wrap the beef around each egg to fully cover the egg with beef.
3. Prepare three bowls: 1) with flour, 2) egg whisked with milk, and 3) breadcrumbs. Dredge each egg in flour, dip in egg then roll in breadcrumbs. Refrigerate Scotch eggs for 20 minutes.
4. Spray Cook & Crisp Basket with cooking spray. Add scotch eggs on basket in a single layer. Place basket in pot
5. Close the lid and move the slider to AIR FRY/HOB. Select AIR FRY, set the temperature to 190°C, and set the time to 8 minutes. Press START/STOP to begin cooking. flip and AIR FRY for more 7 minutes.

Standing Rib Roast

Prep Time	Cook Time	Total Time	Serving Size
5 Minutes	*1H15 Mins*	*1H40 Mins*	*4 servings*

INGREDIENTS

- 2 kg standing rib roast/prime rib
- 3 tbsp olive oil
- Salt & pepper to taste
- 1 tsp smoked paprika
- 1 tsp garlic powder
- 10 garlic cloves, minced
- ½ tsp dried rosemary
- ½ tsp dried thyme

Steps

1. Rub the standing rib roast with oil, then sprinkle with salt & pepper, paprika, and garlic powder.
2. Cover the standing rib roast with minced garlic, rosemary and thyme.
3. Place the standing rib roast in greased Cook & Crisp Basket, Place basket in pot.
4. Close the lid and move the slider to AIR FRY/HOB. Select AIR FRY, set the temperature to 190°C, and set the time to 20 minutes. Press START/STOP to begin cooking , flipping halfway through cooking time.
5. Reduce heat to 157°C and continue to Air fry for more 50 mins for medium-rare.
6. Let the standing rib roast rest for 30 mins, then slice and serve.

Birmingham Balti

Prep Time	Cook Time	Total Time	Serving Size
10 Minutes	*30 Minutes*	*40 Minutes*	*4 servings*

INGREDIENTS

- 2 tbsp oil
- 600g lamb shoulder, cubed
- 2 onions, chopped
- 4 carrots, thickly sliced
- 3 garlic cloves, minced
- 2 tsp grated ginger
- 2 green chillies, deseeded, finely chopped
- 1 tbsp garam masala
- 2 tsp ground cumin
- Handful fresh coriander, finely chopped
- 375g tin chopped tomatoes
- 100ml lamb stock
- 375ml coconut milk

Steps

1. Move the slider to AIR FRY/HOB. Select SEAR/SAUTÉ and set the temperature to 5. Select START/STOP, add oil, brown lamb in batches and transfer to bowl. Add more oil, cook onions and carrots until softened. Add all ingredients to Ninja Foodi pot.
2. Close lid and cook on high pressure for 25 mins. Let pressure release naturally. Select Start/Stop to begin cooking. Move slider to Air Fry/HOB to unlock the lid, then carefully open it. Serve hot.

Baby Back Ribs

Prep Time *5 Minutes* | **Cook Time** *35 Minutes* | **Total Time** *40 Minutes* | **Serving Size** *4 servings*

INGREDIENTS

- 1 ½ kg baby back ribs
- 1 tbsp brown sugar
- 1 tbsp white sugar
- 2 tsp smoked paprika
- 1 tsp garlic powder
- ½ tsp ground black pepper
- ½ tsp ground cumin
- ½ tsp onion powder
- 80ml barbeque sauce

Steps

1. Remove membrane from the ribs. Cut ribs into 4 portions.
2. In a small bowl, add all seasonings. Rub seasonings mixture all over ribs. Place ribs in Ninja Cook & Crisp basket. Add 350ml water to bottom of Ninja Foodi. Place basket in Ninja.
3. Close the lid with valve is in the seal position and move the slider to COMBI-STEAM. Select Steam & Roast set temperature to 170°C, and time to 35 minutes. Select Start/Stop to begin cooking.Flipping halfway through cooking time.
4. Brush with barbeque sauce, then Roast for another 5 minutes. Serve

Toad In The Hole

Prep Time *10 Minutes* | **Cook Time** *30 Minutes* | **Total Time** *40 Minutes* | **Serving Size** *4 servings*

INGREDIENTS

- 450g English sausages, slightly browned

Batter:

- 180g plain flour
- 340ml milk
- 2 tbsp butter
- 3 eggs
- ¼ tsp baking powder
- Pinch salt

Steps

1. In a large bowl, add all batter ingredients. Whisk until combined and smooth.
2. Grease 23 x 23-cm baking dish. Put sausages in the dish, and pour the batter over sausages.
3. Add 350ml water to bottom of Ninja Foodi. Place bottom layer of Deluxe Reversible Rack in the lower position. Place the dish on top of rack, then place rack in the pot.
4. Close the lid with valve is in the seal position and move the slider to COMBI-STEAM. Select Steam & Bake set temperature to 180°C, and time to 30 minutes. Select Start/Stop to begin cooking. Serve.

Beef Roast

Prep Time 10 *Minutes* | Cook Time 45 *Minutes* | Total Time 55 *Mins* | Serving Size 6 *servings*

INGREDIENTS

- 1.5kg rolled British beef topside joint
- 1 tbsp oil
- 1 sprig fresh rosemary
- 1 sprig fresh thyme
- Salt & pepper to taste
- 2 tbsp light brown sugar
- 2 tsp dried oregano
- 1 tsp paprika

Steps

1. Rub roast with oil then season roast with seasoning.
2. Move the slider to AIR FRY/HOB. Select SEAR/SAUTÉ and set the temperature to HI-5. Select START/STOP, add oil, add beef and sear on all sides. Transfer to a plate.
3. Add 250ml water to bottom of Ninja Foodi. Place bottom layer of Deluxe Reversible Rack in the lower position. Place the beef on top of rack, then place rack in the ninja pot.
4. Close the lid with valve is in the seal position and move the slider to COMBI-STEAM. Select Steam ROAST set temperature to 190°C, and time to 20 minutes. Select Start/Stop to begin cooking.
5. After 20 mins, turn down heat to 170°C roast for 30 mins until centre of beef reads 52°C on a probe.
6. Once cooked, let it rest for 15 mins, loosely covered with foil then slice and serve.

Meatloaf

Prep Time *5 Minutes*

Cook Time *55 Minutes*

Total Time *1 Hour*

Serving Size *5 servings*

INGREDIENTS

- 1 onion, finely chopped
- 2 garlic cloves, minced
- 500g beef mince
- 1 egg
- 75g breadcrumbs
- Salt & pepper to taste
- 75ml milk
- 1 tbsp Worcestershire sauce
- 1 tbsp chopped parsley
- 1 tbsp dried oregano
- 1 tbsp thyme
- 1 tbsp tomato purée

Steps

1. In bowl, add all ingredients. Mix and shape the mixture into a loaf shape. Put on a greased baking that will fit in your ninja.
2. Add 250ml water to bottom of Ninja Foodi. Place bottom layer of Deluxe Reversible Rack in the lower position. Place the tray on top of rack, then place rack in the ninja pot.
3. Close the lid with valve is in the seal position and move the slider to COMBI-STEAM. Select Steam bake set temperature to 155°C, and time to 50-55 minutes. Select Start/Stop to begin cooking.
4. Carefully remove meatloaf and let Rest for 5 minutes, still on its tray. Slice and serve with potatoes.

Rosemary Garlic Lamp Chops

Prep Time
5 Minutes

Cook Time
15 Minutes

Total Time
20 Minutes

Serving Size
2 servings

INGREDIENTS

- 600g lamb chops , about 7-8 chops
- 3 tbsp oil
- 2 tbsp chopped rosemary
- 1 tsp garlic powder
- Salt & pepper to taste

Steps

1. Pat dry the lamb chops.
2. In a large bowl, add all ingredients and mix to coat lamp chops with seasoning. Cover and refrigerate for 1 hour.
3. Add 250ml water to bottom of Ninja Foodi. Place bottom layer of Deluxe Reversible Rack in the lower position. Cover with foil, then add chops in a single layer. place rack in the ninja pot.
4. Close the lid with valve is in the seal position and move the slider to COMBI-STEAM. Select Steam bake set temperature to 195°C, and time to 15 minutes. Select Start/Stop to begin cooking , flipping halfway through cooking time.

Garlic Butter Steak

Prep Time
12 Minutes

Cook Time
18 Minutes

Total Time
30 Minutes

Serving Size
2 servings

INGREDIENTS

- 2 (170g each) steaks, (2cm thick, rinsed & patted dry)
- 1 tsp. oil
- ½ tsp. garlic powder
- Butter
- Salt & pepper to taste

Steps

1. Coat steaks with oil. Season both sides with garlic powder, salt & pepper.
2. Add 250ml water to bottom of Ninja Foodi. Place the bottom layer of the reversible rack in the lower position in the pot. Cover with foil, then add steaks in a single layer. place rack in the ninja pot.
3. Close the lid with valve is in the seal position and move the slider to COMBI-STEAM. Select Steam bake set temperature to 185°C, and time to 31 minutes. Select Start/Stop to begin cooking , flipping halfway through cooking time.
4. Remove from ninja, add some butter on top of steak, cover with foil and allow to rest for 4 mins. Serve .

Stuffed Meat Loaf

Prep Time
30 Minutes

Cook Time
15 Minutes

Total Time
35 Minutes

Serving Size
6 servings

INGREDIENTS

For the Meatloaf

1 large egg, lightly beaten
- 20g breadcrumbs
- 1 tsp salt
- 400g minced beef

For the Filling

- 420g mashed potatoes (with milk and butter)
- 2 hard-boiled large eggs, chopped
- 140g mayonnaise
- 50g grated Parmesan cheese
- 225g chopped celery
- 1 green onion, chopped
- Salt & pepper to taste

Steps

1. In a large bowl, mix all filling ingredients.
2. In a bowl, add beaten egg, bread crumbs and salt. Add beef; mix. On a large piece of foil, pat mixture into a 35x20-cm. rectangle. Spread filling over top to within 2.5cm. of edges. Roll up, starting with a short side, removing foil as you roll. Seal ends; place on a large plate. Refrigerate, covered, overnight.
3. Cut roll into 6 slices. Add slices on Cook & Crisp Basket in a single layer. Place basket in Ninja Foodi.
4. Close the lid and move the slider to AIR FRY/HOB. Select AIR FRY, set the temperature to 162°C, and set the time to 15-20 minutes. Press START/STOP to begin cooking.

Mongolian Beef

Prep Time
30 Minutes

Cook Time
10 Minutes

Total Time
40 Minutes

Serving Size
4 servings

INGREDIENTS

- 450g Flank/Bavette or Ramp Steak, thinly sliced
- 40g cornflour
- 2 tsp oil
- 1/2 tsp ground ginger
- 1 garlic clove, minced
- 120ml soy sauce
- 120ml water
- 150g brown sugar

Steps

1. Coat steak slices with cornflour. Add steak slices to Ninja Cook & Crisp basket.
2. Close the lid and move the slider to AIR FRY/HOB. Select AIR FRY, set the temperature to 198°C, and set the time to 10 minutes. Press START/STOP to begin cooking. Flipping halfway through cooking time.
3. In a saucepan on medium high heat, add ginger, garlic, oil, soy sauce, water and brown sugar. Stir until combined. Bring to a gentle boil, then remove from heat.
4. Add cooked steak slices in a bowl, pour over the sauce and let set for 5 mins.

Sausage Rolls

Prep Time	Cook Time	Total Time	Serving Size
15 Minutes	*25 Minutes*	*40 Minutes*	*4 servings*

INGREDIENTS

- 2 tbsp oil
- 1 onion, finely chopped
- 6 higher-welfare sausages
- 4 tbsp breadcrumbs
- 250g puff pastry
- 1 egg mixed with 4 tbsp milk

Steps

1. Move the slider to AIR FRY/HOB. Select SEAR/SAUTÉ and set the temperature to low. Select START/STOP, add oil, and cook onion until soft and golden.
2. With a sharp knife, cut skin of sausages and take meat out. Add it in bowl with sauteed and breadcrumbs. Then mix well with hands until combined.
3. Roll pastry out into a big rectangle on a floured surface and cut it lengthways to 2 long rectangles. Roll the meat into sausage shapes and lay it in the centre of each rectangle.
4. Brush pastry with egg/water mixture, then fold one side of the pastry over, wrapping the filling inside. Press down with edge of a spoon to seal. Cut into pieces and brush with egg wash.
5. Add sausage rolls on Cook & Crisp Basket in a single layer. Place basket in Ninja Foodi.
6. Close the lid and move the slider to AIR FRY/HOB. Select AIR FRY, set the temperature to 180°C/350°F, and set the time to 25 minutes. Press START/STOP to begin cooking.

Hash Browns Bake

Prep Time	Cook Time	Total Time	Serving Size
15 Minutes	*30 Minutes*	*30 Minutes*	*4 servings*

INGREDIENTS

- 400g minced beef or turkey
- 1 small onion, chopped
- Salt & pepper to taste
- 480g frozen mini hash browns
- 120ml chicken stock
- 3 tbsp plain flour
- 2 tbsp melted butter
- 120ml milk
- 70g grated cheddar cheese

Steps

1. Grease baking dish that will fit 20cm baking dish.
2. Move the slider to AIR FRY/HOB. Select SEAR/SAUTÉ and set the temperature to 4. Select START/STOP, add oil, brown beef and onion. Season with salt & pepper.
3. Transfer to beef to prepared baking dish, top with hash browns. In a bowl, add stock, milk, butter and flour, mix & pour over hash browns. Sprinkle with cheese.
4. Add 250ml water to bottom of Ninja Foodi. Place bottom layer of Deluxe Reversible Rack in the lower position. Place the baking dish on top of rack, then place rack in the ninja pot.
5. Close the lid with valve is in the seal position and move the slider to COMBI-STEAM. Select Steam bake set temperature to 180°C, and time to 30 minutes. Select Start/Stop to begin cooking.

Spaghetti Bolognese

INGREDIENTS

- 300g dried spaghetti
- 250g minced beef
- 1 onion , chopped
- 3 garlic cloves , minced
- 1 celery stalk , chopped
- A pinch dried oregano
- A pinch dried basil
- 2 tbsp oil , divided
- 240ml chicken stock
- 500ml water
- 156ml tomato paste
- 2 tbsp soy sauce
- 1 tbsp Worcestershire sauce
- Salt & pepper to taste

Steps

1. Move the slider to AIR FRY/HOB. Select SEAR/SAUTÉ and set the temperature to HI-5. Select START/STOP to preheat Ninja foodi for 5 minutes.
2. Add 1 tbsp oil to Ninja. Add mince and cook until browned, then transfer to a plate.
3. Add remaining oil and add onion, celery and cook until softened. Add garlic and stir until fragrant. Add all remaining ingredients and season with salt and pepper. Stir, scrapping the bottom of the pot. Split the spaghetti in half and add them into the ninja inner pot.
4. Close the lid with valve is in the seal position and move the slider to pressure. Cook on high for 6 minutes. Select DELAYED RELEASE and set time for 5 mins. Select Start/Stop to begin cooking.
5. Move slider to Air Fry/HOB to unlock the lid, then carefully open it. Stir and serve hot topped with grated cheese.

Bangers and Mash

Prep Time	Cook Time	Total Time	Serving Size
15 Minutes	*25 Minutes*	*40 Minutes*	*3 servings*

INGREDIENTS

- 500g small potatoes
- 500g sausages
- 4 tbsp unsalted butter, divided
- 4 tbsp double cream
- 1 onion, cut into slices
- 200ml beef stock
- 1 tsp Worcestershire sauce
- 1 tbsp balsamic vinegar
- 1 tbsp cornflour mixed with 1 tbsp water
- Salt & pepper to taste

Steps

1. In your Ninja Foodi, add potatoes and water. Add sausage on top in a single layer.
2. Close the lid with valve is in the seal position and move the slider to pressure. Cook on high for 10 minutes. Use the arrows to select PRESSURE RELEASE and select QUICK RELEASE. Select Start/Stop to begin cooking.
3. Move slider to Air Fry/HOB to unlock the lid, then carefully open it. Transfer sausage to a plate and transfer potatoes into a bowl.
4. Add the double cream, 60g butter, salt & pepper to the potatoes. Use a potato masher to mash the potatoes to the desired consistency. (add more salt and double cream if necessary).
5. Move the slider to AIR FRY/HOB. Select SEAR/SAUTÉ and set the temperature to HI-5. Select START/STOP to preheat Ninja foodi for 5 minutes.
6. Add 2 tbsp butter Ninja Foodi pot. Then add onions. Sauté until onions softened and brown, for 4 minutes. Pour in the Worcestershire sauce and balsamic vinegar and stir.
7. Pour stock along with cornflour/water mixture. Whisk until it begins to thicken. Season with salt and pepper.
8. Plate the mashed potatoes, sausages, and gravy. Serve immediately.

Chicken Pot Pie

Prep Time	Cook Time	Total Time	Serving Size
10 *Minutes*	30 *Minutes*	40 *Minutes*	4 *servings*

INGREDIENTS

Pie Crust

- 300g plain flour
- 1 tsp salt
- 270g unsalted butter, (cut into small cubes)
- 5 to 6 tbsp iced water

Pie Filling

- 75g plus 1 tbsp unsalted butter, divided
- 1 onion, (diced)
- 1 celery stalk, (chopped)
- 125ml chicken stock
- 2 large boneless skinless chicken breasts, (cut into bite-size pieces)
- 2 large potatoes, (cut into 2.5cm cubes)
- 1/4 tsp dried thyme
- 140g frozen peas and carrots
- 50g plain flour
- 125ml milk, plus more as needed
- Salt & pepper to taste

Steps

1. In a large mixing bowl, add flour & salt. Mix until combined. Add the butter into the flour mixture, Mash with fork until resembles very coarse meal. Gradually add water until dough just sticks together into ball.
2. Move the slider to AIR FRY/HOB. Select SEAR/SAUTÉ and set the temperature to HI-5. Select START/STOP to preheat Ninja foodi for 5 minutes.
3. Add the 1 tbsp butter to Ninja. Add onion, celery and sauté for 3 minutes, until tender. Add chicken stock, chicken, potatoes, thyme, and season with salt & pepper.
4. Close the lid with valve is in the seal position and move the slider to pressure. Cook on high for 3 minutes. Select Start/Stop to begin cooking. Use the arrows to select PRESSURE RELEASE and select QUICK RELEASE. Select Start/Stop to begin cooking.
5. Move slider to Air Fry/HOB to unlock the lid, then carefully open it.
6. Add the peas and carrots. Whisk in remaining butter and flour. Cook for 3 minutes, until bubbly. Gradually add milk, stirring for 2 more minutes, until the sauce is thick and creamy.
7. Grease a deep-dish pie. Transfer the pie crust into floured surface and roll it into a circle that's at least 2.5cm larger than the baking dish.
8. Pour chicken mixture into the pie dish. Top with the pie crust (poke some holes in the crust top).
9. Add 250ml water to bottom of Ninja Foodi. Place bottom layer of Deluxe Reversible Rack in the lower position. Place the pie dish on top of rack, then place rack in the ninja pot.
10. Close the lid with valve is in the seal position and move the slider to COMBI-STEAM. Select Steam & Bake set temperature to 190°C, and time to 15 minutes. Select Start/Stop to begin cooking.

Cornish chicken pasties

INGREDIENTS

Prep Time	Cook Time	Total Time	Serving Size
10 *Minutes*	40 *Minutes*	50 *Minutes*	8 *servings*

Pasties

- 500g plain flour
- 250g cold butter
- 1 egg , beaten for brushing
- 150ml water

Filling

- 1 swede, finely chopped
- 1 onion, , finely chopped
- 1 carrot, finely chopped
- 1 celery stalk, finely chopped
- 2 boneless skinless chicken breasts, (cut into 1-cm pieces)
- 60g plain flour
- 1 tsp mustard seeds
- 120g grated cheddar cheese
- 60ml melted butter
- Salt & pepper to taste

Steps

1. In a large bowl, add all filling ingredients, mix, then set aside.
2. In a large mixing bowl, add flour & salt. Mix until combined. Add the butter into the flour mixture, Mash with fork until resembles very coarse meal. Gradually add water until dough just sticks together into ball. Do not over mix.
3. Divide dough into 8 equal balls. Transfer into a floured, then roll out each pastry to 20-cm circle. Repeat until you have 8 circles.
4. Fill each pastie with even amount of filling on one side of each pastry circle and brush edges with beaten egg. Fold top half of the pasty down over the filling, pressing down to seal with your thumb to press down and seal around the edges. Brush pasties tops with egg.
5. Place pasties in Foodi Cook & Crisp basket. Place basket in Ninja Foodi.
6. Close the lid and move the slider to AIR FRY/HOB. Select AIR FRY, set the temperature to 190°C, and set the time to 35 minutes. Press START/STOP to begin cooking. Flip halfway through cooking time. Check pasties if they`re not done cook for more 5-8 Minutes.
7. Serve.

Chicken Parmo

Prep Time	Cook Time	Total Time	Serving Size
5 Minutes	*15 Minutes*	*20 Minutes*	*4 servings*

INGREDIENTS

- 3 chicken breasts halves, skinless and boneless
- 60g plain flour
- 2 eggs
- 150g breadcrumbs
- 1 tsp basil, chopped
- 500g grated parmesan

Topping:

- 25g butter
- 25g plain flour
- 250ml milk
- 1 bay leaf
- 75g grated parmesan cheese
- 50g mature cheddar cheese

Steps

1. Pound the chicken breasts into thinner pieces that are the same thickness.
2. In a bowl, add flour, salt, and pepper. In another bowl, beat eggs. In a third bowl, mix together the breadcrumbs, basil, and Parmesan.
3. Coat chicken in flour mixture, then in egg and finally cover in breadcrumbs until coated. Repeat for all chicken breasts.
4. Add Cook & Crisp basket in Ninaj Foodi and place chicken in basket in single layer.
5. Close the lid and move the slider to AIR FRY/HOB. Select AIR FRY, set the temperature to 180°C, and set the time to 10 minutes. Press START/STOP to begin cooking. Flipping halfway through cooking time
6. In a saucepan over medium heat, melt butter, add the flour; stir until smooth. Remove from heat; gradually whisk in the milk. Return to heat, add bay leaf and bring to boil, stirring for 5 minutes until thick. Season with salt & pepper. Set aside.
7. Move the slider to AIR FRY/HOB, Open lid, top chicken with sauce then cheddar and Parmesan cheese.
8. Close Lid. Select AIR FRY, set the temperature to 180°C, and set the time to 5 minutes. Press START/STOP to begin cooking.
9. When cooking time is done, Serve with pasta.

Chicken mushroom pie

Prep Time	Cook Time	Total Time	Serving Size
5 Minutes	*15 Minutes*	*30 Minutes*	*4 servings*

INGREDIENTS

- 500g skinless boneless chicken thighs
- 2 tbsp oil
- 4 scallions, chopped
- 350g mushrooms
- 320g sheet puff pastry
- 600ml milk
- 1 tablespoon plain flour
- 1 tablespoon wholegrain mustard

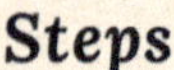

Steps

1. Move the slider to AIR FRY/HOB. Select SEAR/SAUTÉ and set the temperature to 4. Add oil, scallions, mushrooms and sauté for 6 minutes, stirring regularly.
2. Add milk, chicken, and season with salt & pepper.
3. Close the lid with valve is in the seal position and move the slider to pressure. Cook on high for 3 minutes and select QUICK RELEASE. Select Start/Stop to begin cooking.
4. Open lid. Move the slider to AIR FRY/HOB. Select SEAR/SAUTÉ and set the temperature to 3, whisk in flour. Cook for 3 minutes, until bubbly and the sauce is thick and creamy.
5. Grease a pie dish that will fit in your ninja foodi. Transfer chicken mixture into the pie dish.
6. Top with the puff pastry (poke some holes in the crust top).
7. Add 250ml water to bottom of Ninja Foodi. Place bottom layer of Deluxe Reversible Rack in the lower position. Place the pie dish on top of rack, then place rack in the ninja pot.
8. Close the lid with valve is in the seal position and move the slider to COMBI-STEAM. Select Steam & Bake set temperature to 190°C, and time to 15 minutes. Select Start/Stop to begin cooking.

Chicken Tikka Masala

Prep Time	Cook Time	Total Time	Serving Size
10 *Minutes*	25 *Minutes*	35 *Minutes*	4 *servings*

INGREDIENTS

- 4 boneless, skinless chicken thighs, cut into chunks
- 1 onion, finely chopped
- 1 garlic clove, minced
- 1 tsp ginger, finely grated
- 2 tbsp tikka curry paste
- 50ml double cream
- 240ml tinned crushed tomatoes
- 1/2 tbsp vinegar
- 1/2 tbsp light brown soft sugar
- 1/2 cinnamon stick
- 2 cardamom pods
- Salt & pepper to taste

Steps

1. Move the slider to AIR FRY/HOB. Select SEAR/SAUTÉ and set the temperature to HI-5. Select START/STOP to preheat Ninja foodi for 5 minutes. Add onions and sauté until soft. Add chicken pieces and cook until browned on all sides. Add all ingredients into Ninja pot except double cream. Stir.
2. Close the lid with valve is in seal position and move slider to pressure. Cook on high for 8 minutes. Use the arrows to select PRESSURE RELEASE, select QUICK RELEASE. Select Start/Stop to begin cooking.
3. Move slider to AIR FRY/HOB. Select SEAR/SAUTÉ and set to medium heat. Add cream and adjust seasoning, stir until slightly thickens. serve with rice.

Chicken Rice Casserole

Prep Time	Cook Time	Total Time	Serving Size
15 *Minutes*	10 *Minutes*	25 *Minutes*	5 *servings*

INGREDIENTS

- 5 skinless chicken thighs
- 1 onion , chopped
- 2 garlic cloves, minced
- 2 tbsp oil
- 300g uncooked long grain rice
- 400ml hot chicken stock
- 300ml hot water
- 1 tsp smoked paprika
- 1 tsp dried thyme
- 1/2 tsp garlic powder
- 1/2 tsp onion powder
- 1 carrot, grated
- Salt & pepper to taste

Steps

1. Move the slider to AIR FRY/HOB. Select SEAR/SAUTÉ and set the temperature to HI-5. Select START/STOP. Add oil. Season chicken with seasoning on both sides. Add chicken to ninja inner pot and cook until browned on all sides. Remove chicken and set aside.
2. Add rice, onion, garlic, rice, stock, carrots and season with salt and pepper. Stir. Place the Reversible Rack in the lower position into cooking pot. Place top tier on Rack. Place chicken on rack and close lid.
3. Move the slider to the COMBI-STEAM. Select STEAM MEALS. Cook at 180°C for 9 minutes. Select Start/Stop to begin cooking.
4. Open lid, let set for 5 minutes, then remove chicken and fluff up rice. Serve.

Chicken, Broccoli Rice

Prep Time	Cook Time	Total Time	Serving Size
10 Minutes	*25 Minutes*	*35 Minutes*	*4 servings*

INGREDIENTS

- 450 boneless skinless chicken, cut into 2.5-cm pieces
- 300g broccoli florets
- 1 small onion , chopped
- 3 tbsp oil
- 1/2 tsp garlic powder
- 1 tbsp grated fresh ginger
- 1 tbsp soy sauce
- Salt & pepper to taste
- 200g long grain rice, rinsed and drained
- 400ml water
- 1 tbsp melted butter
- ½ tsp salt

Steps

1. Add all ingredients except broccoli in the bottom of the pot. Stir together.
2. Place the bottom layer of the reversible rack in the lower position in the pot. Cover with foil, then add broccoli florets.
3. Close the lid and move the slider to the COMBI-STEAM position. Select STEAM MEALS, set temperature to 200°C, and set time to 6 minutes. Press START/STOP to begin.
4. When cooking is complete, carefully remove the entire rack with broccoli.
5. Fluff the rice and chicken. Then serve with broccoli.

Honey Mustard Chicken Breasts

Prep Time	Cook Time	Total Time	Serving Size
10 Minutes	*25 Minutes*	*35 Minutes*	*4 servings*

INGREDIENTS

- 2 tbsp melted butter
- 85g honey
- 60g English mustard
- 1 tbsp oil
- 2 tsp fresh lemon juice
- salt & pepper to taste
- 4 boneless skinless chicken breasts

Steps

1. In a bowl, add butter, honey, mustard, oil, and lemon juice. Season with salt and pepper. Transfer half of the honey mustard mixture to a separate bowl for later.
2. Pound down the chicken 2.5cm thick. Brush both sides of the chicken with honey mustard and place it in Ninja Cook & Crisp basket.
3. Close the lid and move the slider to AIR FRY/HOB. Select AIR FRY, set the temperature to 193°C, and set the time to 12 minutes. Press START/STOP to begin cooking. Flipping halfway through cooking time, flipping halfway through cooking time. serve with remaining sauce.

Hunters Chicken

Prep Time	Cook Time	Total Time	Serving Size
10 *Minutes*	30 *Minutes*	35 *Minutes*	*4 servings*

INGREDIENTS

- 4 chicken breasts
- 8 strips streaky beef bacon
- 240ml BBQ sauce
- 60g grated cheddar cheese
- 60g grated mozzarella cheese
- Salt & pepper to taste

Steps

1. Wrap each chicken breast in two strips of bacon.
2. Transfer chicken to a baking dish that will fit in your ninja. Place bottom layer of Deluxe Reversible Rack in the lower position. Place the baking dish on top of rack, then place rack in the ninja.
3. Close the and move the slider to AIR FRY/HOB. Select AIR FRY and set temperature to 190° C. Set time for 25 minutes. Press START/STOP to begin cooking.
4. Remove the baking dish from the Ninja Foodi. Spoon the BBQ sauce on chicken, then sprinkle with cheese.Close the and move the slider to AIR FRY/HOB. Select AIR FRY and set temperature to 190° C. Set time for 5 minutes. Press START/STOP to begin cooking.
5. Open lid, serve with mash and vegetables.

Roasted Turkey Breast

Prep Time	Cook Time	Total Time	Serving Size
5 *Minutes*	45 *Minutes*	50 Minutes	10 *servings*

INGREDIENTS

- 2 kg turkey breast, bone & skin in, room temperature
- 1 tbsp olive oil
- 2 tsps salt
- 1 tsp paprika
- 1 tsp garlic powder
- 1 tsp dried oregano
- 1 tsp dried thyme
- ½ tsp black pepper

Steps

1. Rub oil all over the turkey breast. Season both sides with seasoning.
2. Add 350ml water to bottom of Ninja Foodi. Add Foodi Cook & Crisp basket in. Place the turkey, skin side down, into the basket.
3. Close the lid with valve in seal position and move slider to COMBI-STEAM. Select Steam & Crisp set temperature to 180°C, and time to 45 minutes. Select Start/Stop to begin cooking. Flipping halfway through cooking time.
4. Remove breast from ninja drawer and let rest 10 minutes loosely covered with foil before carving.

Pizza Stuffed Chicken Thighs

Prep Time	Cook Time	Total Time	Serving Size
10 Minutes	*15 Minutes*	*35 Minutes*	*4 servings*

INGREDIENTS

- 4-5 boneless skinless chicken thighs
- 125g pizza sauce
- 14 slices pepperoni
- ½ small onion sliced
- 145g sliced mozzarella cheese
- 60g grated parmesan cheese for topping
- Salt & pepper to taste

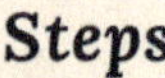

Steps

1. Place chicken thighs in between 2 pieces of baking paper. Pound chicken to create a thin piece. Spread a spoonful pizza sauce on each chicken piece. Add cheese, 4 pepperoni slices, and onion slices on top.
2. Fold one side of the chicken over onto the other and hold chicken together with a toothpick.
3. Line ninja Cook & Crisp basket with baking paper and place chicken in basket.
4. Close the lid and move the slider to AIR FRY/HOB. Select AIR FRY, set the temperature to 190°C, and set the time to 12 minutes. Press START/STOP to begin cooking. Flipping halfway through cooking time
5. Add cheese on the top of the chicken and air fry for more 2 minutes.

Apricot Chicken

Prep Time	Cook Time	Total Time	Serving Size
10 Minutes	*15 Minutes*	*35 Minutes*	*4 servings*

INGREDIENTS

- 100g apricot preserves
- 60g chili sauce
- 1 tbsp mustard
- 4 boneless skinless chicken breast halves, 115g each
- Salt & pepper to taste

Steps

1. In a saucepan over medium-low heat, combine preserves, chili sauce, and mustard. Stir and heat.
2. Pound the thicker end of each chicken breast to even it out. Pat chicken dry with a paper towel. Spray with oil and rub to coat. Sprinkle with salt & pepper.
3. Place chicken in Ninja Cook & Crisp basket.
4. Close the lid and move the slider to AIR FRY/HOB. Select AIR FRY, set the temperature to 190°C, and set the time to 10 minutes. Press START/STOP to begin cooking.Flipping chicken and brush with sauce half way through cooking time.
5. Let chicken rest for 10 minutes, then slice and serve.

Grilled Chicken Skewers

Prep Time	Cook Time	Total Time	Serving Size
30 *Minutes*	18 *Minutes*	*45 Minutes*	*4 servings*

INGREDIENTS

- 450g boneless, skinless chicken breasts, cut into 2.5cm cubes
- 2 tbsp soy sauce
- 1/4 tsp of : onion powder, smoked paprika, and sage.
- 1 tbsp oil
- Salt & pepper to taste

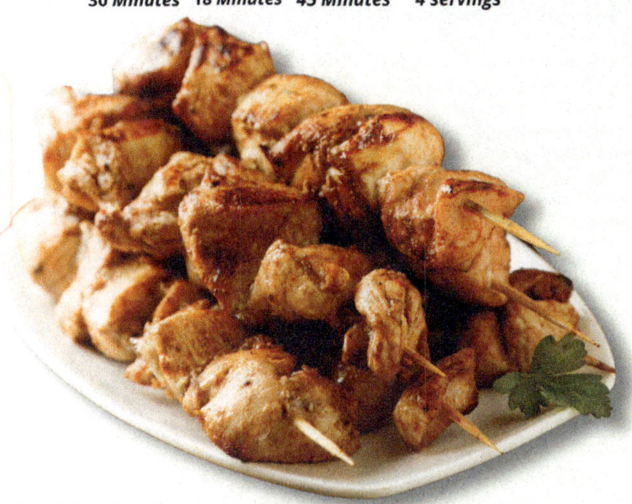

Steps

1. In a bowl, add all ingredients, mix. Cover the bowl. Marinate for 30 mins in the refrigerator.
2. Remove the chicken and thread it onto a skewers.
3. Transfer chicken into greased Deluxe Reversible Rack. Place rack into Ninja.
4. Close the and move the slider to AIR FRY/HOB. Select AIR FRY and set temperature to 180° C. Set time for 18 minutes. Press START/STOP to begin cooking. Flip halfway through cooking time.
5. Serve.

Cornish Game Hens

Prep Time	Cook Time	Total Time	Serving Size
5 *Minutes*	45 *Minutes*	50 Minutes	4 *servings*

INGREDIENTS

- 2 cornish hens, (700g each)
- 2 tbsp olive oil
- 2 tbsp fresh rosemary, chopped
- 1 tsp garlic powder
- 1 tsp paprika
- 1 tbsp lemon juice
- Salt & pepper to taste

Steps

1. In a medium bowl, mix all of the seasonings. Brush hens with oil and coat with seasonings.
2. Put the hens breast side down into greased Deluxe Reversible Rack. Place rack into Ninja.
3. Close the and move the slider to AIR FRY/HOB. Select AIR FRY and set temperature to 180° C. Set time for 45 minutes. Press START/STOP to begin cooking. (Remove rack half way through cook time and flip chicken.)
4. Open lid, remove from Ninja, let the hen rest for 11 minutes before carving.

Baked Chicken & Gravy

Prep Time	Cook Time	Total Time	Serving Size
5 Minutes	*45 Minutes*	*50 Minutes*	*5 servings*

INGREDIENTS

- 1.25 kgbone in, skin on chicken thighs
- 2 tsp oil
- 1 tsp smoked paprika
- 1 tsp dried thyme
- 1 tsp garlic powder

Gravy:
- 4 tbsp plain flour
- 360ml beef stock
- Salt & pepper to taste

Steps

1. Rub chicken with oil, then sprinkle with spices. Make sure to coat chicken all over with spices.
2. Place the chicken skin into a 23x33cm baking dish.
3. In a bowl, add gravy ingredients and whisk until combined. Pour into baking dish around the chicken.
4. Add 350ml water to bottom of Ninja Foodi. Place bottom layer of Deluxe Reversible Rack in the lower position. Place the dish on top of rack, then place rack in the ninja pot.
5. Close the lid with valve is in the seal position and move the slider to COMBI-STEAM. Select Steam & Bake set temperature to 180°C, and time to 35-45 minutes. Select Start/Stop to begin cooking.
6. When done, Remove chicken onto a plate, then whisk the gravy until smooth.
7. Serve gravy with chicken

Chicken Stew

Prep Time	Cook Time	Total Time	Serving Size
10 Minutes	*10 Minutes*	*20 Minutes*	*4 servings*

INGREDIENTS

- 8 chicken drumsticks
- 2 potatoes, peeled & cubed
- 4 garlic cloves, minced
- 1 onion, chopped
- Salt & pepper to taste
- 400ml chicken stock
- 3 carrots , cut thick
- 4 celery stalks , chopped
- 2 tbsp tomato concentrate
- 2 tsp Worscestershire sauce

Steps

1. Move the slider to AIR FRY/HOB. Select SEAR/SAUTÉ and set the temperature to 5. Select START/STOP, add oil, chicken cook until browned. Add all remaining ingredients. stir, scrapping the bottom of the pot to loose any stuck pieces.
2. Close the lid with valve in seal position and move slider to pressure. Cook on high for 10 minutes.Then Use the arrows to select PRESSURE RELEASE and Select DELAYED RELEASE and set time for 5 mins. Select Start/Stop to begin cooking.
3. Move the slider to AIR FRY/HOB. Open lid and serve.

Creamy Chicken Soup

 **Prep Time** *15 Minutes*

 **Cook Time** *45 Minutes*

 **Total Time** 1 Hour

 **Serving Size** *8 servings*

INGREDIENTS

- 2 tablespoons Oil
- 1 onion, chopped
- 2 celery stalks, chopped
- 2 carrots, chopped
- 5 garlic cloves, minced
- 1 litre Chicken Stock, divided
- 1 kg chicken breast, boneless, skinless
- 4 tablespoons plain flour
- 120ml double cream
- Salt & pepper to taste

Steps

1. Move the slider to AIR FRY/HOB. Select SEAR/SAUTÉ and set the temperature to 4. Select START/STOP, add oil, onion, carrots, and celery. once softened add garlic. cook until fragrant. Cancel the SEAR/SAUTÉ. Add chicken and 700ml stock, salt & pepper.
2. Close lid and cook on high pressure for 15 mins. Select DELAYED RELEASE and set time for 10 mins. Select Start/Stop to begin cooking.
3. In a bowl, whisk remaining stock with the flour.
4. When cooking time is finished. Move the slider to AIR FRY/HOB. Select SEAR/SAUTÉ and set the temperature to 3. Open lid, Slowly pour the stock/flour mixture, while stirring until thickened, about 5 minutes. Serve.

Chicken & Rice Soup

 **Prep Time** *10 Minutes*

 **Cook Time** *15 Minutes*

 **Total Time** *25 Minutes*

 **Serving Size** *5 servings*

INGREDIENTS

- 2 tbspoil
- 2 large boneless skinless chicken breasts cut into small pieces
- 1 onion diced
- 3 carrots, peeled and diced
- 3 celery stalks thinly sliced
- 4 garlic cloves, minced
- 500ml chicken stock
- 1 1/2 tsp. dried oregano
- 1 bay leaf
- Salt & pepper to taste
- 200ml double cream
- 350g cooked rice

Steps

1. Move the slider to AIR FRY/HOB. Select SEAR/SAUTÉ and set the temperature to 4. Select START/STOP, heat the oil. add onion, carrots, and celery. Add garlic and cook, stirring constantly, until fragrant. Add stock, chicken, salt, pepper, oregano, and bay leaf.
2. Close lid and Cook on high pressure for 10 mins. Select QUICK RELEASE. Select Start/Stop to begin cooking.
3. Move the slider to AIR FRY/HOB. Select SEAR/SAUTÉ, Add the double cream and rice, and cook, stirring occasionally, until rice is heated through.
4. Season with additional salt to taste. Serve in bowls and top with fresh coriander, if desired.

Butter Chicken

Prep Time	**Cook Time**	**Total Time**	**Serving Size**
10 *Minutes*	20 *Minutes*	30 *Minutes*	8 *servings*

INGREDIENTS

- 1 kg boneless, skinless chicken thighs
- 2 tsp. oil
- 1 onion, chopped
- 6 garlic cloves, crushed
- 1 tbsp fresh grated ginger
- 2 tbsp tomato concentrate
- 300g chopped tomato
- 1 tbsp. garam masala
- 2 tsp. turmeric
- Salt & pepper to taste
- ½ tsp. cumin
- 1/4 tsp. cinnamon
- 125ml chicken stock
- 170g long grain rice, rinsed and drained
- 240ml water
- 60g butter
- 120g double cream
- 150g plain yogurt

Steps

1. Select SEAR/SAUTÉ, set on med, and add oil. Once hot, add garlic and ginger and cook, stirring, until fragrant. Add Tomato puree, tomato concentrate, garam masala, turmeric, salt, pepper and cumin and cook for 3 minutes, stirring occasionally.
2. Turn off the SEAR/SAUTÉ and add the cinnamon , chicken stock and stir. Add chicken breasts.
3. Place bottom layer of Deluxe Reversible Rack in the lower position over the chicken and place a 18cm baking pan on top. Add the rice and water to the pan . Place rack in ninja foodi.
4. Close the lid with valve is in the seal position and move the slider to pressure. Cook on high for 12 minutes. Select QUICK RELEASE. Select Start/Stop to begin cooking.
5. Open the lid and Remove the rice and the rack. Ruffle the rice, cover to keep warm and set aside. Remove chicken and dice then into cubes and set aside.
6. Select SEAR/SAUTÉ, set on 3 and add the butter, yogurt and cream and cook until they thicken slightly, about 2 minutes. Add the diced chicken to the Ninja Foodi pot to heat.
7. Serve the chicken with the rice and garnish with coriander leaf, if desired.

Tandoori Chicken

Prep Time	Cook Time	Total Time	Serving Size
4 Minutes	*6 Minutes*	*10 Minutes*	*4 servings*

INGREDIENTS

- 700g boneless chicken thighs, cut into chunks
- 250g yogurt
- 2 tsp grated fresh ginger
- 1 tsp cumin
- 1 tsp chilli powder
- 1 tsp lemon juice
- 3 tsp garam masala
- 2 garlic cloves, minced
- 1 tsp oil
- 2 drops red gel food coloring
- Salt & pepper to taste

Steps

1. In a bowl, add all ingredients and mix together until chicken coated in the marinade. cover and refrigerate for at least 1 hour.
2. Add the chicken Into Ninja Cook & Crisp basket.
3. Close the lid and move the slider to AIR FRY/HOB. Select AIR FRY, set the temperature to 200°C, and set the time to 15 minutes.Press START/STOP to begin cooking. Flip halfway through cooking time.
4. Serve.

BBQ Chicken Legs

Prep Time	Cook Time	Total Time	Serving Size
5 Minutes	*15 Minutes*	*20 Minutes*	*4 servings*

INGREDIENTS

- 8 chicken legs
- 2 tsp smoked paprika
- 125ml BBQ sauce
- 1 tsp onion powder
- Salt & pepper to taste

Steps

1. Season chicken legs with salt, pepper and paprika.
2. Add the chicken Into Ninja Cook & Crisp basket in a single layer .
3. Close the lid and move the slider to AIR FRY/HOB. Select AIR FRY, set the temperature to 180°C, and set the time to 15-20 minutes.Press START/STOP to begin cooking. Flip halfway through cooking time.
4. Brush each chicken leg with BBQ sauce. Air Fry for more 2 mins.

Stuffed Chicken Breast

Prep Time
10 Minutes

Cook Time
20 Minutes

Total Time
30 Minutes

Serving Size
4 servings

INGREDIENTS

- 2 chicken breasts
- 120g swiss cheese/gouda slices
- 200 Salami
- 1 egg, (beaten)
- 100g breadcrumbs
- 1 tbsp garlic powder
- 1 tbsp onion powder
- 1 tbsp butter, melted
- salt & pepper to taste

Steps

1. On a chopping board, Cut chicken breasts in half horizontally through the middle. place a chicken breast between two sheets of clingfilm wrap, pound until about ½cm thik. Season with salt & pepper.
2. Put 3 cheese slices, 4 salami on each chicken breast. Roll chicken, secure with toothpicks.
3. In a dish, mix breadcrumbs & seasoning. Roll chicken in beaten egg, coat with breadcrumbs.
4. Add chicken in single layer inside of Ninja Cook & Crisp basket, brush with butter.
5. Close the lid and move the slider to AIR FRY/HOB. Select AIR FRY, set the temperature to 180°C, and set the time to 20 minutes.Press START/STOP to begin cooking. Flip halfway through cooking time.
6. Remove from Ninja and serve.

Balsamic chicken

Prep Time
10 Minutes

Cook Time
15 Minutes

Total Time
25 Minutes

Serving Size
4 servings

INGREDIENTS

- 8 chicken thigh cutlets, skin on

Balsamic Sauce:

- 80ml balsamic vinegar
- 60ml soy sauce
- 60ml tomato sauce
- 3 garlic cloves, crushed
- 60ml chicken stock
- 2 tbsp honey
- Salt & pepper to taste

Steps

1. Select SEAR/SAUTÉ, set on HI, add oil. Once hot, add chicken skin side down first and cook, until golden brown. Remove from ninja foodi and set aside.
2. In a bowl, mix all sauce ingredients. Pour into ninja foodi and stir, scrapping the bottom of pot to make sure there is no stuck pieces. Add back the chicken.
3. Close the lid with valve is in the seal position. Cook on high pressure for 10 mins. Select Quick Release.
4. Open lid, serve the chicken with Balsamic sauce.

Fish and Chips

INGREDIENTS

- 900g white fish fillets
- 60g plain flour + 100g plain flour, divided
- 30g cornsflour
- 1 tbsp sugar
- 120ml cold water
- 1 egg
- 100g breadcrumbs
- Salt & pepper to taste

For the chips

- 1 kg, peeled and cut into 1.5cm long chips
- Salt & pepper to taste

Steps

1. Soak potatoes in a bowl of cold water for 30 minutes.
2. In a bowl, whisk 60g flour and cornflour. In another bowl, stir together 100g flour, garlic powder, onion powder, salt, pepper, and Bicarbonate of soda. Pour in cold water and stir to combine. (if too thick add more water)
3. Dredge each fish piece in flour mixture, then in the batter. Place the fish pieces back in the flour mixture to fully coat.
4. Line ninja Cook & Crisp basket with baking paper and spray with cooking spray. add fish into basket. Spray tops of fish with cooking spray. Add basket in Ninja Foodi.
5. Close the lid and move the slider to AIR FRY/HOB. Select AIR FRY, set the temperature to 190°C, and set the time to 10 minutes. Press START/STOP to begin cooking. Flipping halfway through cooking time.
6. Remove from ninja, transfer to a plate and cover with foil. Set aside.
7. Add potatoes to Cook & Crisp basket. Close the lid and move the slider to AIR FRY/HOB. Select AIR FRY, set the temperature to 190°C, and set the time to 14 minutes until golden brown and crispy. Press START/STOP to begin cooking. Flipping halfway through cooking time.
8. Serve the fish and chips.

Creamy Fish Pie

Prep Time	Cook Time	Total Time	Serving Size
10 *Minutes*	20 *Minutes*	50 *Minutes*	6 *servings*

INGREDIENTS

- 1 kg maris piper potatoes , peeled and chopped
- 250ml water
- 4 tbsp butter
- 4tbsp double cream
- 500ml milk
- 2 salmon fillets, boneless
- 2 haddock fillet, boneless
- 15 prawns, devained
- 40g plain flour
- 180g grated cheddar cheese
- Salt & pepper to taste

Steps

1. Put the potatoes, water and salt in Ninja Foodi pot.
2. Close the lid with valve is in the seal position and move the slider to pressure. Cook on high for 7 minutes. Use the arrows to select PRESSURE RELEASE and select QUICK RELEASE. Select Start/Stop to begin cooking.
3. Move slider to Air Fry/HOB to unlock the lid, then carefully open it.
4. Drain potatoes and transfer to a bowl, add butter, double cream, salt, pepper to taste. Mash and cover. Wipe out pot and return to Ninja.
5. Move the slider to AIR FRY/HOB. Select SEAR/SAUTÉ and set the temperature to 4. Select START/STOP, add oil, add flour and sauté for 1 minute. Gradually stir in milk, cook for a few minutes until thickened.
6. Select SEAR/SAUTÉ and set to 3, add salmon, haddock, prawns, season with salt & pepper and simmer for 3 minutes. Top with the mashed potatoes, and sprinkle with cheddar cheese.
7. Close the lid and move the slider to AIR FRY/HOB. Select AIR FRY, set the temperature to 180°C, and set the time to 30 minutes. Press START/STOP to begin cooking.
8. Remove from Ninja. Let stand for 5 minutes before serving.

Prawn & Tomato Stew

Prep Time	Cook Time	Total Time	Serving Size
2 Minutes	*5 Minutes*	*8 Minutes*	*6 servings*

INGREDIENTS

- 1 garlic clove, crushed
- 1 onion, chopped
- 300g tinned chopped tomatoes
- 240ml stock
- ½ tsp turmeric powder
- 450g Prawn, peeled and deveined
- ½ tsp ground coriander, ground
- ½ tsp dried thyme
- Salt & pepper to taste

Steps

1. Select SEAR/SAUTÉ, set temp to 4, add oil, onion, garlic. Sauté for 2 mins. Add all remaining ingredients.
2. Close the lid with valve is in the seal position and move the slider to pressure. Cook on high for 3 minutes. Use the arrows to select PRESSURE RELEASE and select QUICK RELEASE. Select Start/Stop to begin cooking.
3. Open lid, adjust seasoning and stir. Serve topped with fresh coriander.

Cornish crab bisque

Prep Time	Cook Time	Total Time	Serving Size
7 Minutes	*13 Minutes*	*20 Minutes*	*6 servings*

INGREDIENTS

- 2 tbsp oil
- 1 onion, chopped
- 1 fennel bulb, chopped
- 1 carrot, chopped
- 1 bay leaves
- 1 garlic clove, crushed
- 3 tbsp tomato concentrate
- 200g fresh crabmeat
- 1 liter fish stock
- 120ml double cream
- 1 zest lemon
- 1 tbsp lemon juice
- Salt & pepper to taste

Steps

1. Select SEAR/SAUTÉ, set set temp to 4 , add oil. Add fennel, onion, and carrots and saute for 5 minutes, add garlic and cook for 1 min. Add remaining ingredients (except double cream). Mix until combined.
2. Close the lid with valve is in the seal position and move the slider to pressure. Cook on high for 13 minutes. Use the arrows to select PRESSURE RELEASE and select QUICK RELEASE. Select Start/Stop to begin cooking.
3. Open the lid, add the double cream. Stir until combined. Blend with blender until smooth.

Prawn Fajitas

Prep Time	Cook Time	Total Time	Serving Size
5 Minutes	*20 Minutes*	*25 Minutes*	*4 servings*

INGREDIENTS

- 900g medium prawn, peeled
- 2 red bell pepper, (sliced)
- 1 green bell pepper, (sliced)
- 1 onion, (sliced)
- Salt & pepper to taste
- ½ tsp onion powder
- ½ tsp garlic powder
- ½ tsp ground cumin
- ½ tsp smoked paprika
- Salt & Pepper to taste

Steps

1. Add the peppers, onion, and seasoning into a bowl, mix.
2. Add Foodi Cook & Crisp basket in ninja, add prawns, peppers, and onion inside of Ninja Foodi basket.
3. Close the and move the slider to AIR FRY/HOB. Select AIR FRY and set temperature to 195°C. Set time for 11 minutes. Press START/STOP to begin cooking.
4. Open lid and add the prawn. Spray it with cooking spray and mix together. AIR FRY for another 10 minutes. Stirring halfway through cooking time.

Cullen Skink

Prep Time	Cook Time	Total Time	Serving Size
5 Minutes	*15 Minutes*	*20 Minutes*	*4 servings*

INGREDIENTS

- 1 onion, (chopped)
- 2 leeks, (chopped)
- 2 potatoes, (peeled & chopped)
- 200g Neeps, (chopped)
- 1 tbsp oil
- 375g Haddock
- 600ml fish stock
- 200ml whole milk
- 2 tsp thyme
- 1 tbsp parsley, (chopped)
- Salt & pepper to taste

Steps

1. Select SEAR/SAUTÉ, and set to 4, add oil, onion, leek, potatoes, neeps and sauté for 3 minutes. Add Haddock, fish stock, thyme and salt & pepper and stir.
2. Close the lid with valve is in the seal position and move the slider to pressure. Cook on high for 8 mins. Use the arrows to select PRESSURE RELEASE and select QUICK RELEASE. Select Start/Stop to begin cooking.
3. Open the lid, Remove the Haddock, add milk. Stir. Blend with blender until smooth.
4. Transfer into bowls then serve topped with Haddock and parsley.

Prawn Tacos

Prep Time *5 Minutes* | **Cook Time** *8 Minutes* | **Total Time** *15 Minutes* | **Serving Size** *4 servings*

INGREDIENTS

- 450g small prawn raw, peeled, deveined, tails-off
- 1 tbsp oil
- ¾ tsp chili powder
- ¾ tsp garlic powder
- ½ tsp cumin
- ½ tsp onion powder
- Salt & pepper to taste

Toppings:

- 4 flour tortillas or corn tortillas
- green shredded cabbage
- sliced avocados
- crumbled feta cheese
- lime

Steps

1. In a bowl. mix prawn with oil, chili powder, garlic powder, cumin, onion powder, salt & pepper.
2. Add Foodi Cook & Crisp basket in ninja, add prawns inside of Ninja Foodi basket.
3. Close the and move the slider to AIR FRY/HOB. Select AIR FRY and set temperature to 190°C. Set time for 8 minutes. Press START/STOP to begin cooking.
4. Assemble tortillas with prawn, cabbage, and cheese. serve.

Bermuda Fish Chowder

Prep Time *12 Minutes* | **Cook Time** *6 Minutes* | **Total Time** *18 Minutes* | **Serving Size** *4 servings*

INGREDIENTS

- 500ml chicken stock
- 1 (450g) tin chopped tomatoes
- 80ml ketchup
- 3 potatoes, peeled & cubed
- 1 onion, chopped
- 2 celery, chopped
- 2 large carrots, chopped
- 2 ½ tsp Worcestershire sauce
- 3 garlic cloves, crushed
- 2 bay leaves
- ¼ tsp ground cloves
- 1 tsp curry powder
- 500g fish fillets, chopped
- Salt & pepper to taste

Steps

1. In your Ninja Foodi, add all ingredients. (except fish)
2. Close the lid with valve is in the seal position and move the slider to pressure. Cook on high for 5 minutes. Use the arrows to select PRESSURE RELEASE and select QUICK RELEASE. Select Start/Stop to begin cooking.
3. Open the lid. Add fish. close lid and cook on high pressure for another 3 mins. Use the arrows to select PRESSURE RELEASE and select QUICK RELEASE. Select Start/Stop to begin cooking.
4. Open the lid, stir.Transfer into bowls then serve.

Creamy Cayenne Prawns

Prep Time	Cook Time	Total Time	Serving Size
5 Minutes	*10 Minutes*	*15 Minutes*	*4 servings*

INGREDIENTS

- 500g prawns, (shelled)
- 1 tbsp oil
- 1 tbsp butter
- 2 garlic clove, (minced)
- 3/4 tsp cayenne
- 200ml chicken/fish stock
- 200ml double cream
- Salt & pepper to taste

Steps

1. Move the slider to AIR FRY/HOB. Select SEAR/SAUTÉ and set the temperature to HI-5. Select START/STOP, add butter & oil. When hot, add prawns, garlic, & cayenne, sauté for 2 mins. Add stock and stir.
2. Close the lid with valve is in the seal position and move the slider to pressure. Cook on high for 3 mins. Use the arrows to select PRESSURE RELEASE and select QUICK RELEASE. Select Start/Stop to begin cooking.
3. Open the lid & select saute. Add cream, stir and simmer for a minute.
4. Serve with rice or potato mash.

Honey Lemon Prawns

Prep Time	Cook Time	Total Time	Serving Size
30 Minutes	*5 Minutes*	*35 Minutes*	*2 servings*

INGREDIENTS

- 450g large Prawns raw; shell and tail removed
- 1 ½ tbsp oil
- 1 ½ tbsp lemon juice
- 1 ½ tbsp honey
- 2 cloves garlic minced
- Salt & pepper to taste

Steps

1. In a large bowl, stir oil, lemon juice, honey, garlic and salt. Add prawns, marinate for 30 mins.
2. Shake excess marinade off prawns.
3. Add Foodi Cook & Crisp basket in ninja, add prawns inside of Ninja Foodi basket. Coat with cooking spray.
4. Close the and move the slider to AIR FRY/HOB. Select AIR FRY and set temperature to 200°C. Set time for 5 minutes. Press START/STOP to begin cooking. Flipping and spraying with cooking spray halfway through cooking time.

Maple-Dijon Glaze Salmon

Prep Time
4 Minutes

Cook Time
15 Minutes

Total Time
20 Minutes

Serving Size
4 servings

INGREDIENTS

- 1 tbsp oil
- 4 salmon fillets

Maple-Dijon Glaze:

- 3 tbsp butter
- 3 tbsp golden/Mable syrup
- 1 tbsp Dijon mustard
- 1 lemon juiced
- 1 garlic clove, minced
- Salt & pepper to taste

Steps

1. Drizzle oil over salmon; season with salt & pepper.
2. Add Foodi Cook & Crisp basket in ninja, add salmons inside of Ninja Foodi basket.
3. Close the and move the slider to AIR FRY/HOB. Select AIR FRY and set temperature to 200°C. Set time for 6 minutes. Press START/STOP to begin cooking.
4. In a saucepan over medium heat, add all glaze ingredients and stir for 2 minutes until thickens.
5. Drizzle salmon fillets with glaze right before serving.

Fish Chowder

Prep Time
10 Minutes

Cook Time
20 Minutes

Total Time
30 Minutes

Serving Size
8 servings

INGREDIENTS

- 1 onion, chopped
- 4 celery stalks, chopped
- 450g potatoes, peeled & chopped
- 1 litre vegetable stock
- 160g corn kernels
- 450g cod
- 2 tablespoons cornflour mixed with 2 tbsp water
- 240ml double cream
- 1 teaspoon garlic powder
- 1 teaspoon dried thyme
- Salt to taste

Steps

1. Add onion, celery, and potatoes. Then pour in stock then corn. Place cod fillets on top .
2. Close the lid with valve is in the seal position and move the slider to pressure. Cook on high for 5 mins. Select DELAYED RELEASE and set time for 10 mins. Select Start/Stop to begin cooking.
3. Open lid, Move the slider to AIR FRY/HOB. Select SEAR/SAUTÉ and set the temperature to 4. Select START/STOP, and bring to a boil. Add cornflour/water mixture to the ninja, mixing in until thickened, press "Cancel". Then add in the double cream, garlic powder, thyme, and salt and mix.
4. Remove from ninja and serve.

Tuna Burgers

Prep Time	Cook Time	Total Time	Serving Size
8 Minutes	*12 Minutes*	*20 Minutes*	*4 servings*

INGREDIENTS

- 1 egg, beaten
- 50g breadcrumbs
- Handful finely chopped celery
- 80ml mayonnaise
- 1 small onion, finely chopped
- 200g tinned light tuna in water, drained
- Salt & pepper to taste

Steps

1. In a large bowl, combine all ingredients. Shape into 4 patties.
2. Place patties in Ninja Cook & Crisp basket. place basket in ninja.
3. Close lid and move the slider to AIR FRY/HOB. Select AIR FRY and set temperature to 177° C. Set time for 12 minutes. Press START/STOP to begin cooking. (Flipping halfway through cooking time).

Lemon Pepper Baked Cod

Prep Time	Cook Time	Total Time	Serving Size
2\5 *Minutes*	10 *Minutes*	15 *Minutes*	*4 servings*

INGREDIENTS

- 4 cod fillets (225g each)
- 1 ½ tablespoons oil
- ¼ teaspoon garlic powder
- ¼ teaspoon onion powder
- ¼ tablespoon dried oregano
- ¼ tablespoon dried thyme
- ¼ teaspoon paprika
- 1 teaspoon lemon zest
- Salt & pepper to taste

Steps

1. In a bowl, combine all the seasoning. Rub cod fillets with oil then coat with seasoning.
2. Add 240ml water to bottom of Ninja Foodi. Place the bottom layer of the reversible rack in the lower position in the pot. Cover with foil, then add cod fillets.
3. Close the lid with valve is in the seal position and move the slider to COMBI-STEAM. Select Steam & Bake set temperature to 190°C, and time to 10 minutes until the fish flakes easily with a fork at it's thickest point. Select Start/Stop to begin cooking.
4. Serve with fresh lemon juice.

Crispy Fish Fillets

Prep Time	Cook Time	Total Time	Serving Size
5 Minutes	*15 Minutes*	*20 Minutes*	*4 servings*

INGREDIENTS

- 450g white fish fillets (1.5cm thick)
- 1 egg
- 60g yellow cornmeal
- 1 tsp paprika
- ½ tsp garlic powder
- Salt & pepper to taste

Steps

1. Prepare two bowls: 1) cornmeal and seasonings 2) beaten egg. Dip each fish fillet in egg then roll in cornmeal mixture.
2. Place fish into Ninja Cook & Crisp basket in a single layer . Spray with cooking spray.
3. Air Fry at 200°C for 10 minutes, flip halfway through cooking time. If its not fully cooked, return to air fryer and cook 7 minutes.
4. Once done, squeeze with lemon. Serve immediately.

Parmesan Crusted Salmon

Prep Time	Cook Time	Total Time	Serving Size
5 Minutes	*8 Minutes*	*13 Minutes*	*2 servings*

INGREDIENTS

- 2 salmon fillets
- 60g mayonnaise
- 1 tsp of each (garlic powder, onion powder, dried basil, dried oregano and dried thyme)
- shredded parmesan cheese to taste

Steps

1. In a bowl, mix mayonnaise, and herbs.
2. Place the salmon in Ninja Cook & Crisp basket.
3. Spread the herb mayonnaise mixture on the top of salmon fillets. Top with parmesan cheese.
4. Air Fry at 175°C for 8 minutes.

Prawn & Vegetables

Prep Time	Cook Time	Total Time	Serving Size
25 Minutes	*20 Minutes*	*45 Minutes*	*4 servings*

INGREDIENTS

- 300g Small prawn Peeled & Deveined
- 1 bag of frozen mixed Vegetables
- 1 Tbsp Cajun Seasoning or your favourite seasoning mix

Steps

1. Add the prawn and vegetables to a large bowl.
2. Top it with Cajun seasoning and spray with cooking spray. Mix.
3. Place the prawn and vegetables in Ninja Cook & Crisp basket in a single layer.
4. Air Fry at 180°C for 10 minutes.
5. Open lid and mix prawn and vegetables.
6. Air Fry for an additional 10 minutes.
7. Serve over rice.

Coconut Prawns

Prep Time	Cook Time	Total Time	Serving Size
30 Minutes	*15 Minutes*	*45 Minutes*	*6 servings*

INGREDIENTS

- 60g plain flour
- 2 eggs
- 50g unsweetened shredded coconut
- 50g breadcrumbs
- 350g uncooked prawn, peeled and deveined
- Salt & pepper to taste

Steps

1. Prepare three bowls: 1) flour, salt & pepper 2) Beaten egg 3) Coconut & Breadcrumbs. Dredge each prawn in flour, dip in egg then roll in coconut/breadcrumb mixture.
2. Place prawn on a plate. Coat prawn with cooking spray.
3. Place the prawn in Ninja Cook & Crisp basket in a single layer.
4. Air Fry at 200°C for 6 minutes. Flipping halfway through cooking time.

Lentil Soup

Prep Time	Cook Time	Total Time	Serving Size
5 Minutes	*40 Minutes*	*45 Minutes*	*4 servings*

INGREDIENTS

- 2 tbs. olive oil
- 1 onion, chopped
- 2 carrots, chopped
- 2 celery stalks, thinly sliced
- 4 garlic cloves, minced
- 1 tsp. dried sage
- 800g tin chopped tomatoes
- 200g dry brown/green lentils
- 1 liter vegetable stock
- ½ tsp. dried thyme
- 4 potatoes, cut into 1.5cm cubes
- Salt & pepper to taste

Steps

1. Move the slider to AIR FRY/HOB. Select SEAR/SAUTÉ and set the temperature to 4. Select START/STOP, heat oil. add onion, carrots, and celery. Sauté for 6 minutes . Add garlic and sage, stir into veggies, and sauté for a minute. cancel Sauté. Add potatoes, tinned tomatoes, lentils, and vegetable stock. Stir.
2. Secure lid with valve in seal position. Cook on high pressure for 15 minutes. When time is up, let the pressure release naturally.
3. Open the lid. Serve the soup in bowls.

Cauliflower Soup

Prep Time	Cook Time	Total Time	Serving Size
15 Minutes	*15 Minutes*	*30 Minutes*	*8 servings*

Good.

INGREDIENTS

- 1 tbsp. oil
- 1 onion, diced
- 3 cloves garlic, minced
- 2 carrots, chopped
- 600g cauliflower, chopped
- 1.5 litre chicken stock
- 120ml double cream
- 4 tbsp. Cornflour
- 150 ~~120g~~ Grated cheddar cheese
- Salt & pepper to taste

Steps

1. Move the slider to AIR FRY/HOB. Select SEAR/SAUTÉ and set the temperature to 4. Select START/STOP, heat oil. add onion. Sauté until soft. Add garlic. Add chicken stock and deglaze the bottom. Add the carrots and the cauliflower.
2. PRESSURE Secure lid with valve in seal position. Cook on high pressure for 5 minutes. Select quick release.
3. In a small mixing bowl, stir together the cream and Cornflour .
4. Open lid, Move the slider to AIR FRY/HOB. Select SEAR/SAUTÉ . Pour cream/Cornflour mixture into soup. Bring to a simmer for about 5 minutes until slightly thickened.
5. Stir in the Grated cheese until melted. Season with salt to taste. Serve.

Liquidise remainder when cool

Leek & Potato Soup

Prep Time	Cook Time	Total Time	Serving Size
10 Minutes	*15 Minutes*	*20 Minutes*	*6 servings*

INGREDIENTS

- 3 tbsp Butter
- 1 tbsp Oil
- 2 large Leeks, (chopped)
- 1 small Onion, (chopped)
- 2 Garlic Cloves, (minced)
- 6 small Potatoes
- 1 liter Chicken Stock
- 100ml Milk
- 150ml Double Cream
- Salt & Pepper to taste

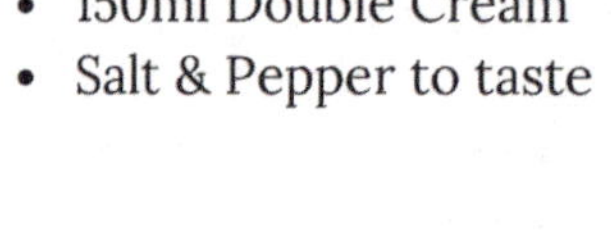

Steps

1. Move the slider to AIR FRY/HOB. Select SEAR/SAUTÉ and set the temperature to 4. Select START/STOP, Add the oil. When the oil is hot, add the onion, leeks and garlic, sauté for 3 mins.
2. Add potatoes and saute for another 7 mins. Add the stock and milk. Stir.
3. Secure lid with valve in seal position. Cook on high for 6 mins. Select QUICK RELEASE. Select Start/Stop to begin cooking.
4. Open the lid, add cream, season with salt & pepper. Blend the soup, using a hand blender.
5. Transfer into bowls and serve.

Squash Soup

Prep Time	Cook Time	Total Time	Serving Size
10 Minutes	*10 Minutes*	*20 Minutes*	*6 servings*

INGREDIENTS

- 1200g butternut squash, peeled, cut into 2.5cm pieces
- 2 medium carrots, cut into 2.5cm pieces
- 1 large onion, cut into 1 cm-thick wedges
- 2 cloves garlic
- 1 Jalapeno Pepper, seeded
- 4 sprigs fresh thyme
- 150ml double cream
- 1 litre chicken stock
- Salt & Pepper to taste

Steps

1. Add all ingredients except double cream to ninja foodi inner pot.
2. Secure lid with valve in seal position. Cook on high for 8 mins. Select QUICK RELEASE. Select Start/Stop to begin cooking.
3. Open lid, add double cream. Use a hand blender to puree until smooth. Transfer into bowls and serve.

Split Yellow Pea Soup

Prep Time	Cook Time	Total Time	Serving Size
5 Minutes	*30 Minutes*	*35 Minutes*	*4 servings*

INGREDIENTS

- 1 tbsp. olive oil
- 1 large onion, chopped
- 2 garlic cloves, chopped
- 1 ½ tsp. finely chopped fresh ginger
- 225g yellow split peas
- 250ml water
- 500ml vegetable stock
- ¾ tsp. ground saffron
- 80ml double cream
- Salt & pepper to taste

Steps

1. Move the slider to AIR FRY/HOB. Select SEAR/SAUTÉ and set the temperature to 4. Select START/STOP, heat oil. add the onion and sauté, stirring constantly,until onion is translucent. Add ginger and garlic, sauté until fragrant. Press Cancel to stop sauté.
2. Add yellow peas, water, vegetable stock, saffron and black pepper and stir.
3. Secure lid with valve in seal position. Cook on high pressure for 15 minutes. Select DELAYED RELEASE and set time for 15 mins. Select Start/Stop to begin cooking.
4. Open the lid, add the double cream and mix. Taste and adjust seasonings. Decorate with chopped coriander leaf and serve.

Tomato & Parmesan soup

Prep Time	Cook Time	Total Time	Serving Size
10 *Minutes*	10 *Minutes*	20 *Minutes*	5 *servings*

INGREDIENTS

- 2 tbsp. butter
- 1 large onion, chopped
- 2 garlic cloves, crushed
- 1 tbsp. dried basil
- 1 tsp. Dried oregano
- 230g softened cream cheese
- 1 liter chicken stock
- One 400g tin whole tomatoes, diced
- Salt & pepper to taste
- 80g grated Parmesan, plus more to garnish

Steps

1. Move the slider to AIR FRY/HOB. Select SEAR/SAUTÉ and set the temperature to 4. Select START/STOP, heat oil. add onions, garlic, basil and oregano and cook until tender. Press Cancel to stop sautéing. Add cream cheese and whisk to soften it. Add stock, tomatoes, Parmesan cheese, salt and pepper.
2. Secure lid with valve in seal position. Cook on high pressure for 8 minutes. Select Quick release
3. Open the lid, and blend with blender until smooth. Taste and adjust the seasoning with salt and pepper.
4. Serve the soup in bowls and garnish with more Parmesan cheese and basil leaves.

Printed in Great Britain
by Amazon